Thomas Wessinghage

Running

Thomas Wessinghage, M.D.

RUNNING

Valuable Advice on
Technique, Training,
Competitive Running, and Sports Medicine

BARRON'S

First English-language edition published in 2001 by Barron's Educational Series, Inc.

Published originally under the title *Laufen*.

© Copyright 1999 by BLV Verlagsgesellschaft mbH, München/Germany.

Translated from the German by Eric A. Bye, M.A. English translation © Copyright 2001 by Barron's Educational Series, Inc.

All inquiries should be addressed to:
Barron's Educational Series, Inc.
250 Wireless Boulevard
Hauppauge, NY 11788
http://www.barronseduc.com

International Standard Book No. 0-7641-1631-2

Library of Congress Catalog Card No. 00-057175

Library of Congress Cataloging-in-Publication Data

Wessinghage, Thomas.
    [Laufen. English]
    Running: detailed advice on equipment, technique, training, competitive running, and sports medicine / Thomas Wessinghage; [translation from the German by Eric A. Bye].
        p. cm.
    Includes index
    ISBN 0-7641-1631-2 (alk. paper)
    1. Running. I. Title.
GV1061.W42 2001
796.42—dc21
00-057175

Printed in Hong Kong
9 8 7 6 5 4 3 2 1

Cover photo: Meinsen and Partners
Cover design: Sander and Krause, Munich
Layout: Anton Walter, Gundelfingen

Photo Credits

L. Adamski-Reek: pp. 15, 21, 31, 57

Bavaria Photo Agency: pp. 6–7, 136–137, 180–181

D. Birkner: p. 19

G. Chai-von der Laage: p. 69

Cologne Sports Academy: p. 148 back

T. Dietschi: p. 45 top

H. Frohlich: pp. 70, 108 top, 112, 113, 173

A. Fromm: pp. 5, 32, 80, 81, 82, 83, 87, 91, 92, 93, 94, 95, 96, 97, 151, 152, 153, 154 top (2x), 160, 161, 162, 163, 164

M. Kestenholz/Keropress: pp. 16, 22–23, 53, 66, 71, 104–105, 110, 126–127, 129

P. Lehmann: pp. 51, 56, 64, 108–109, 111, 124, 125, 133, 140

Polar Deutschland: pp. 29, 39

Puma Schweiz: p. 43

Ryffel Running, Bern: pp. 131, 157

Munich National Antique and Cut Gemstone Collection: p. 10

Erlangen University Library: p. 13

Thomas Wessinghage: pp. 2–3, 8–9, 24, 25, 40, 45 bottom, 63, 78, 79, 84, 85, 98, 99, 100, 101, 135, 148 left (2x), 149, 150, 154 bottom, 156, 167, 168, 169, 173–179

T. Wessinghage/Prof. Glaubitt: p. 177

J. Wirz: pp. 60-61, 138, 139, 142, 145

All graphics by Hellmut Hoffmann, except
Harald and Ruth Bukor: p. 76

Jörg Mair: pp. 18, 28, 36

Preface

Nearly ten years have passed since the first edition of this book was published. Ten years is a very long time for such a popular sport, which is influenced by sports science, medicine, and trends in performance sports and sociology. That is ample reason to bring the book up to date and present it in a new package. The success the book has enjoyed so far justifies that opinion and my decision to keep its fundamental structure intact.

Thomas Wessinghage

Dr. Thomas Wessinghage was born on February 22, 1952 in Hagen, Westfalia, Germany. After graduation in 1970, he began his medical studies in Mainz; that culminated in his qualification exam in 1977. His training in orthopedic medicine led him to Ludenscheid-Hellersen, Los Angeles, and Cologne. In 1988 he became medical director of the North-Central Reha Day Clinic in Norderstedt. He has been the medical director and head physician of the Saarschleife Reha Clinic in Mettlach-Orscholz Germany since 1996.

In the course of his 20-year career as a middle- and long-distance runner, he was named to the German Olympic team four times. He took part in 62 international running events (more than anyone else in the German Track and Field Federation), and he was German champion more than 20 times.

He achieved his greatest success with his 1982 victory in the European 5,000-meter championship. He won the 1,500-meter World Cup in Montreal in 1979, the 1,500-meter Europa Cup in Nice in 1975, and the 5,000 meters in London in 1983. He was the European indoor champion four times at 1,500 meters. He has held various German and

Personal Bests:

800 meters: 1:46.56
1,500 meters: 3:31.58
1 mile: 3:49.98
2,000 meters: 4:52.20
3,000 meters: 7:36.75
5,000 meters: 13:12.78

European records, including 1,500 meters, one mile, and 2,000 meters, which still stood when this book was published. Thomas Wessinghage was selected "Track Runner of the Year" in 1981, and in 1985 he won the Rudolf-Harbig Memorial Award.

Contents

Introduction

Surely there are many types of sports that offer variety and fitness. Running clearly occupies a prominent place among them. You do not need a track or a stadium or any expensive equipment, and you do not have to learn any complicated technique. After a relatively short period of regular training, you feel refreshed, healthy, and more fit than ever before. This increase in spiritual and physical well-being is within everyone's reach. You do not have to be young and athletic to run. There is an appropriate type of running for every performance level, nearly all weight groups, and practically all ages. The positive effects of carefully controlled endurance training have been scientifically confirmed even with beginners in their seventies.

In the last couple of decades, scientists and doctors have been searching for the causes of the ever increasing number of diseases of the heart and circulatory system. Lack of exercise is precisely one of the main reasons for circulatory disorders, blood vessel constriction, and even heart attacks. At the same time, most people know that endurance training is effective in preventing such illnesses. However, few of them realize that there are currently hundreds of outpatient heart-healthy groups nationwide for the treatment and rehabilitation of heart attacks, in which carefully controlled and physician-monitored training is used with success. (Also see page 61.)

Competitive runners obviously have different motives than people who run for health reasons. Competition gives them an opportunity to put their skills to the test. Competing directly against other people or against the clock helps runners see what they can do, increases their self-confidence, and from the standpoint of peace of mind, reduces aggression.

Success in running is not just about health benefits and the possibility of gratifying personal ambition. The social aspect of running sports also plays a big part. All over the country there are hundreds of events where many running enthusiasts of different performance levels get together to practice their sport. A further indication of the

social value of running is found in the tremendous number of participants in citizens' races and marathons. Thousands and thousands of people gather every year for the large marathons in Boston, New York, Frankfurt, and Tokyo, to name but a few. Running is a good sport for the whole family. Since it can be done without great expense of money and time, even families with small children can enjoy running without straining the family budget. Also, many happy marriages have been brought about by the sport, evidently because it affords broad agreement between the partners on some important aspects of their world views. I hope I have convinced you that it is appropriate for you to get involved in sports, especially running. I am confident that you will now find it easier to start running even if you were not convinced before.

Road races have become the most popular type of sport worldwide.

History

The history of running is nearly as old as humanity itself. In prehistoric times, running was a lifesaver in hunting, gathering, and fleeing. Couriers provided relatively quick distribution of information and news.

As the first cultures emerged, recreational types of running were practiced, especially in the upper levels of society. The Egyptian kings Sesotris I and Amenophis II were reputed to be good runners. Solomon (963–925 B.C.) conducted competitions in his courtyard, as did the Hittites, the Sumerians, and the Myceneans.

Running was very highly regarded in archaic and classical Greece (around 800 to 500 B.C. and 500 to 300 B.C., respectively). Homer depicted running competitions in detail in his epics; they were also

Representation of a group of runners on an ancient prize amphora from Athens.

part of funerals, weddings, receptions, and other celebrations. Starting in the ninth century B.C., ritualistic competitions were held at Olympus in honor of Zeus. Starting in 776 B.C., the winners in the Olympic Games were regularly honored.

At first a single run was held over the distance of one stadium (630 feet/192 m). Later on, other disciplines were added, including longer races. Thereafter, the games became very important culturally and politically, and that paid off for the winners in both material and nonmaterial ways. A sacred truce reigned in all of Greece for the duration of the Olympics.

In the classical age and the Hellenistic period that followed it, there developed a class of professional athletes that included some famous runners. The ancient Greeks were aware that the value of running is not restricted to a high-level competitive sport but is important also in education and health. They built gymnasiums with running tracks to educate both the mind and the body. Plato claimed that running was the best of all athletic disciplines. It is also known that the Etruscans, who inhabited the Italian peninsula at the same time, conducted running competitions as part of ritualistic games. They, like so many other tribes of antiquity, had to submit to the military rule of the Romans, who included running as part of their militarily oriented physical education for young males. In addition, Romans incorporated running events in special occasions such as the Spring Runs, in which women also took part.

With the rise of Christianity and under the influence of Hellenistic philosophies, starting around 200 A.D. some tendencies were promoted that worked against physical culture. In 394 A.D. the Eastern Roman Emperor Theodosius the Great abolished the Olympic games, after these "heathenish celebrations" had been in existence for nearly 1,200 years.

Among the Germanic tribes in the early Middle Ages, running ability was a prerequisite for success in war and hunting. Caesar and Tacitus extolled the Germans on account of their speed. Running also played a role in the Germanic songs of gods and heroes, as in the Nibelungenlied with the competition between Siegfried and Hagen and in the Edda with Thor's journey to Utgardloki (ca. 800 to 1250).

From about 1000 to 1300, Europe was dominated by the chivalric culture. In chivalric books of virtue, speed was mentioned as a valuable basic skill. Running competitions were often staged as part of tournaments for knights.

At the same time, in rural areas running events became incorporated into special occasions (such as church consecrations, carnivals, springtime celebrations, and midsummer festivals), and women were eligible to take part. As the chivalric culture inevitably declined with the widespread use of firearms, one consequence was an increased migration of rural customs into the cities. That led to conducting races as parts of carnivals in Nuremberg as early as 1349 and in Vienna starting in 1382; in Augsburg, there were races for women as early as 1448. As part of large shooting contests, there were competitions in Zurich (1456), Augsburg (1470), Rottweil, and Strasbourg; many of the competitions included women.

With the start of the fifteenth century and the development of humanism, attention was again focused on the relationship between people and their physical bodies as well as on other ideas from antiquity. Some initial types of physical education included running. Running was part of the program at Protestant Latin schools and Jesuit schools, usually as part of extracurricular activities.

The development of the sport was quite different in the eighteenth and nineteenth centuries in England. In contrast with the European mainland, the dominant features included the principles of performance, competition, and records. This was a product of Enlightenment thought and was strengthened by the Industrial Revolution.

The sport of running occupied a very important role. The Cotswold Games were held in Barton in 1604; they included running competitions. The nobility enjoyed horse races and running races by the so-called Footmen. This usually involved people in the service of the landed gentry, who competed against one another over distances of 15 or 20 miles (24.1 or 32.2 km). (Starting in 1660 the races were measured in miles.) Considerable bets were placed on the outcome by their masters and the spectators. The Footmen could rightly be considered professional runners. Oftentimes, they ran alone against the clock and frequently had some very impressive finishes. Starting around 1700, English newspapers began reporting on such competitions. So we know about a butcher from that time who achieved a certain degree of fame by running ten miles (16.1 km) in under an hour. (Evidently he acted not in the service of a master, like other runners, but on his own accord and was a professional in today's sense of the word.)

At the start of the nineteenth century, the sport of running found its way into the upper strata of society. Among gentlemen, accepting or demanding money for their performance was of course frowned upon. That helped clear the way for a new era of amateur sports. Universities and colleges were the nurturing ground and stronghold of running. From the middle of the nineteenth century on, races of different lengths were developed, rules were drawn up, and track clubs were founded. The Amateur Athletic Association (AAA) was created in 1880; today it remains the governing association for English track. At around this time the "English" sport crossed over to the mainland and the rest of the world. Sports clubs were founded in Germany, or additional sports were added to the traditional gymnastics clubs. In 1893 the German Amateur Athletic Association was founded in Berlin to promote running sports. Running continued to be integrated more and more into school sports.

Across the water in the New World, the sport of running had a different complexion. As the American Colonies developed, running races—both sprints and long runs— were popular during fairs and holidays as part of an array of recreational events from cooking to eating to racing. Later, racing became a professional sport among lower-class immigrants who benefited from the monetary and social rewards. However, the gambling that also accompanied the sport was abhorrent to the upper classes in America. It was not until the post–Civil War years that amateur running events developed around private clubs and schools. Amateur running divided the classes at first. However, as the upper classes began to get more competitive, they began to recruit runners from the lower classes to their schools and clubs to build their competitions. Running maintained a steady but low profile in American sports until the early 1960s when Dr. Ken Cooper began publishing books that showed that running improved health. The increasing knowledge of the health benefits of running, coupled with Frank

Shorter's Olympic medal in 1972, began a running boom that has never really let go.

For some time in various countries, there had already been movements to revive the Olympic Games of ancient times. The French Baron Pierre de Courbertin, whose primary concern was educational reform, helped the concept of the Olympics become a reality. In 1894, he called a meeting at the Sorbonne in Paris, where it was resolved to revive the Olympic Games. After surmounting great difficulties, the first Olympic Games of the new era were successfully held in Athens in 1896. Paris in 1900 and St. Louis in 1904 were overshadowed by the World's Fairs that took place at the same time, but the fourth games in London in 1908 and the fifth in Stockholm in 1912 came off brilliantly. The spell had been broken.

For decades the Olympic Games have been the highest goal of all athletes, not only runners. Athletes like Owens and Zatopek achieved immortality through their Olympic victories and lent the games brilliance with their performances. Since the end of the seventies, Olympic championships have become increasingly competitive because of the importance of international sports festivals ("Grand Prix" since 1975), the introduction of world track-and-field championships (conducted for the first time in Helsinki in 1983), the steadily increasing number of major international events, and the growing importance of records. Still, an Olympic gold medal is regarded as the highest goal a runner can achieve. Nowadays the Olympic Games have taken on such an importance and—on account of the modern media—have achieved a worldwide presence that threatens to rob them of their identity through the intrigues of power politics and commercial spectacles. In addition, international terrorism constitutes a disturbing threat.

While remaining untouched by all the internal and external problems, or so it seems, performances

"The Race of the Young Journeymen and the Coarse Women," manuscript page from 1509.

keep getting better. More diverse and intense training programs, professionalism in sports, and physiological factors in the athletes (such as acceleration) continually produce new records. The question of where the limits of performance lie can therefore be answered only by saying that they do not exist.

This conclusion surely applies both to men and to women. Until 1968 the longest official distance in championship racing was 800 meters. Since that time there has been a continuous and inevitable tendency to longer distances. Nowadays women have complete access to the realm of extreme endurance races. Women now take part in all types of endurance races in great and increasing numbers—up to the most extreme competitions such as multiple-sport triathlons and ultramarathons.

In the major marathons, the prize money for men's and women's victors has become nearly equal.

However, sport does not mean only high performance. Recreational sports, and especially running, have become an important factor in our lives from a cultural, medical, and financial standpoint.

Changes in the nature of our work, which requires less and less physical effort and thereby causes greater psychological stress, in combination with greater awareness of health issues and increased free time, lead to a search for balance achieved through physical activity. Doctors have long known that by far the greatest majority of health costs are the result of a lack of exercise among people in modern society. The emphasis by some politicians on preventive measures in people's health is a result of facts that have been known since the sixties.

However, nowadays, and starting about three decades ago, millions of runners enjoy their hobby, especially in Europe, North America, and Oceania. Running events that draw 20,000 participants are no longer considered an oddity. Now it seems that since humans have achieved the dream of total mobility that they have harbored for thousands of years, they are again thinking about their original, natural gifts and abilities: health is created only by the continual alternation between exercise and regeneration, activity and recovery.

Running Technique

Movement is life. It externalizes the entire being through body language. People express their feeling of being alive through their posture. Unfortunately, adults who have normal posture and breathing have become exceptions in our technocratic civilization. As they grow up, most people lose the free, unrestricted ways of moving that children and primitive peoples have. Social problems arise when there is a disturbance in people's relationship with movement.

"Back to nature"— in the form of a run through the woods.

Haile Gebreselassie from Ethiopia has perfected the stride of the century in a new era of long-distance running. His world-record runs are always a pleasure to see.

As we become aware of the interplay among the various elements of our bodies when we run, we can succeed in retrieving a part of the naturalness of movement we have lost. That is mainly an issue of proper training that avoids degenerating into a mindless accumulation of miles, as some people see it. Anyone who runs through the woods in the early sunshine and absorbs the sounds and smells of awakening nature knows what we are talking about here.

Running Style

Every human body is a unique, individual biomechanical system. The assumption that any world record holder has the ideal running style for a given distance fails to take into account the vastly different dimensions of each person. Most top-level runners exhibit a great economy of movement: speed and distance covered in running depend on the most economical use of energy. Every runner must try to perfect his or her running style according to this axiom and, without trying to copy world-class athletes, adhere to the fundamental principles that they embody.

It is always important to find the right relationship between exercise and recovery. The stride should be fluid but not too long, the muscles in the hips should be relaxed, the back free from tension, and the upper body inclined slightly forward. The shoulders are relaxed; the arms are free to swing; the elbows are held at approximately a right angle. The hands are slightly open, not clenched in a fist. The head is held erect, and the eyes look straight ahead.

Runners must pay particular attention to the position of their feet. Running is the most basic form of exercise for humans. It is worth remarking that no one was born with shoes on his or her feet. In other words, as we seek a natural running style, people should take their cues from how they run barefoot on a flat, natural surface such as a lawn or a sandy beach. This leads to some surprising discoveries. In this case, without the isolating layer of a shoe sole that is often a half-inch (1.3 cm) thick, runners are forced to resort to the springiness and the cushioning elements inherent in their own bodies. If the middle of the foot around the ball of the little toe is put down first, the lower and upper joint, the knee, and the hip joints are positioned for use and can bring each stride under control with the help of the tensed leg muscles. In this phase, which is referred to as the support phase (where the foot makes contact in front of the body's center of gravity), the main stress is on the outer rim of the leading foot. In the middle support phase (where the foot is located beneath the body's center of gravity), pronation (see below) begins. The stress is now distributed nearly equally on the main joint of the big and little toes and on the heel. In the rear support phase (or push-off phase), the pronation movement is complete. The entire stress is directed in a sequence through the big toe, the bones of the middle of the foot, the inner tarsus, and the shinbone.

Phases in the Motion of Running Barefoot
1. Setting the foot down at the midfoot.
2. Support phase, where the entire foot momentarily makes contact with the surface.
3. Pushing off with the middle of the foot and the first joint of the big toe.

Comparison of stresses to which the foot is subjected upon contact with the ground in the case of runners who first make contact with the heel (above) and those who land on the front of the foot (below). The sharper increase in applied force in the case of heel runners equates to greater stress.

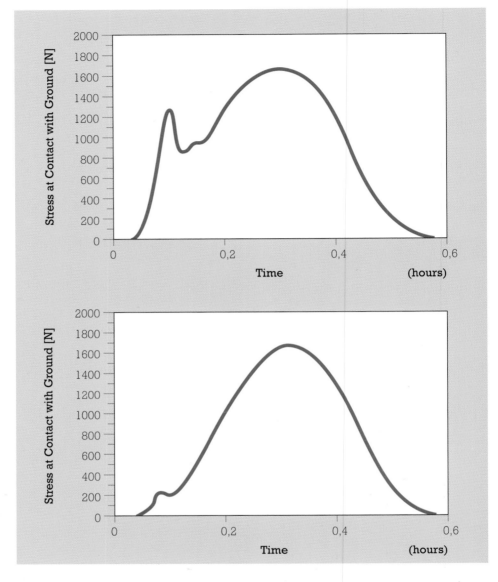

This type of movement is a good deal safer for bones and joints than awkwardly using the heel as a buffer when you touch down in a stride; the heel, after all, is hardly suited to act as a shock absorber. Additionally, this technique affords more speed. In running, pulling with the forward leg (in the early support phase) is more effective than propulsion from the trailing leg (that is, the last part of the support phase). The running style of almost all world-class runners conforms to this basic pattern. Otherwise, there is no cushion provided against shocks to the ankles, knees, hips, and even the spine, which can lead to injuries to muscles (pulls and lumbago) and nerves (ischial disorders).

For every step, forces in the form of kinetic energy amounting to two to three times body weight must be absorbed. In the case of an adult of average weight, that amounts to about 330 to 484 pounds (150 to 220 kg).

18

A running style can be considered to be economical when the body's center of gravity describes the least amount of movement up and down and moves forward in a straight, horizontal line. Making contact with the middle of the foot has another very important effect. Active cushioning of the forces that come to bear shifts the stress in the sensitive structures that are not subject to conditioning by training—the surfaces of the joints—to ones that adapt to training, namely the muscles. Every doctor knows that muscular stress is a good deal easier to treat and has a much better prognosis than does stress to a joint (arthrosis)—from which, as far as we now know, there is no going back. In addition to the foregoing, a possible tendency toward pronation is greatly reduced.

Pronation—What Is It?

Pronation (from the Latin meaning inclining to the front) is a movement in the lower ankle joint. When that occurs, the middle and forward parts of the foot rotate against the back of the foot on an axis that runs diagonally from outside to inside. The heel bone tips inward in what is known as a valgus direction, and the lower leg rotates inward. To the outside observer, it appears that the upper part of the ankle turns inward along with the anklebone.

Pronation is a totally natural movement that is dictated by anatomy. Its extent is the deciding factor in whether it leads to deformities, improper stresses, and eventually to arthrotic changes. Excessive pronation can be fairly noticeable with fallen arches or flat feet. Problems also arise if you have stiff, high arches.

Poor running technique occurs if a person practically falls into each step while running, with a straight knee and heel first approach. There is no choice but for the bones and muscles to cushion the blow, requiring a braking motion, and that uses the ankle tendons as if they were elastic reins—in a way they were never intended to be used. The tendons, shinbone, anklebone, and heel bone are all connected. When they

When people run barefoot, they unconsciously land on the middle of the foot (photo 2) in order to cushion the step. This greatly reduces pronation.

4　　　　　3　　　　　2　　　　　1

are overstretched, they can no longer function to provide lateral stability. As a result, there is a danger of improper stresses on the joints that in the final stages can lead to severe wear and tear: arthrosis. That is why it is important to avoid excessive pronation. Scientific experiments have shown that the painful effects of continued excessive pronation can best be countered by running barefoot, where the middle of the foot is first planted in conjunction with properly tensed muscles. A clean running style is thus more effective and more valuable than the complicated and expensive sole constructions incorporated into many running shoes.

Possible Cause of Pain in the Kneecap

Discomfort in the area of the kneecap may be another reason to pay more attention to running style. The kneecap is momentarily subjected to very great stress when the foot makes contact. It may be susceptible to injury when the thigh muscle (quadriceps femoris) bears on it. There is also a danger of excessive stress on the cartilage on the back of the kneecap. It is less stressful if you first make contact with the middle of the foot. The process is essentially the same, but the force is produced more gradually and gently, and that is better for the knee. A further effect of this "active" running style is that in the swing phase, the foot reaches the most forward point in its movement shortly before it touches the ground. The instant it is planted, it is already moving rearward and pulling the body ahead with the aid of the musculature at the back of the thigh that is used to bend the knee (in the pulling phase). The action of the muscles that straighten the knee is dampened, and pressure on the kneecap is reduced.

Should You Run on the Heel or Ball of Your Foot?

So what should you do if you have been running for years on your heel? As long as you have not been injured and the pronation is fairly limited, you can keep running the same way. It can be very difficult to change styles, for there is often an imbalance between body weight and muscle strength, especially in the calf muscles. In this case, it is a good idea to do some preparatory muscle training (see page 86). This involves regular barefoot running on grass to work on technique and some coordination training (see page 98).

Proper Breathing

Breathing while running should be unconscious and unrestricted. Its rhythm usually establishes itself. Beginners can simply regulate their breathing by counting; that will also keep them from running too fast. If you inhale for four steps and exhale for four (in other words, an eight-step breathing cycle), the pace is not too quick, and the run will be beneficial to your health (see page 61). It is best to breathe through the mouth and the nose; that allows you to breathe as deeply as possible and take in lots of air.

Running Style for Cross-country and Track

For running *uphill*, your stride should be shortened according to the steepness of the grade; push off more forcefully, and swing your arms more intensively to aid your progress. The upper body is inclined forward a little more than when running on level ground. The tempo can be increased in conjunction with the shortened stride. It is important in running uphill to push off from the ankle to take some of the stress off the quadriceps, which have more lifting to do.

Cross-country training.

In running *downhill*, you experience the greatest stress. Mountain climbers know that it is not climbing but, rather, going down a mountain that leads to sore muscles. The same is true for downhill running. It should be controlled very carefully in training. Reduce your cadence, so you glide carefully into the step. The arms should be used to help maintain balance; they may be slightly less bent and held out further than usual from the body. The upper body leans back more than when running on a level surface.

You can use the *cleanest* running style when running on a track. The surface is smooth, level, and consistent. Competitive sprinters use spikes when they run on a track; that encourages running on the front of the foot and provides good traction. It is also possible to use the elasticity of the surface to good advantage in setting up a regular and dynamic stride. When fatigue starts to set in, you can use a technique similar to running uphill: shorten the stride a little, push off more, and use the arms more forcefully. In so doing, the pelvis should be consciously pushed forward a little since when you are tired, you tend to sit back. In other words, you bend at the hips so that your posterior and center of gravity sink lower. Toward the end of the run, when it is time for the kick, you should consciously lift the knees, pick up the tempo, and—just as in running in the hills—push off from the ankles. The quicker this shift takes place, the faster your acceleration. In this changeover, you call on muscle groups that have largely been spared up to this point, and that gives you the strength to finish the run successfully.

Ethiopia was the dominant running nation at the end of the twentieth century.

Equipment

When you run, there is no need to wear anything in particular. Runners are, unlike other athletes, mostly free from conventions; they wear whatever is practical and whatever they like.

Look for comfortable, loose fitting clothing made of materials that breathe so that your body can easily regulate heat. People who live in climates with extremes of heat or cold can benefit from many of the new, technically advanced materials that help keep you warm on cold days and cool on hot days. Most everyone else can find success in just T-shirts and shorts.

Shoes

Shoes are the most important piece of equipment for runners.

There is an incredible variety of running shoes available today. New and supposedly better models are continually being introduced to the market in quick succession, with the support of research and development departments and in cooperation with

Construction features that reduce overpronation:
- *hard midsole material around the inside of the heel;*
- *pronation support under the heel;*
- *heel stabilizer;*
- *stable heel counter (with as tight a fit as possible).*

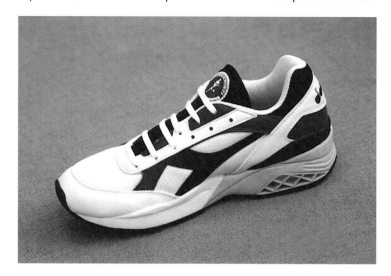

scientific institutes that specialize in biomechanics and materials technology. Consumers find that along with the advantage of a great selection, there comes a difficulty in making the right choice.

In fact, it is very important for every runner to select shoes very carefully. The following little calculation will suffice to demonstrate the point: On average, about 6,500 steps are taken in a 6.2 mile (10 km) run. In every step, forces must be brought under control that amount to two to three times your body weight. For an average-weight westerner, that is between 330 and 484 pounds (150 to 220 kg). That means that every shoe is stressed with a total of 500 to 750 tons in a moderate 6.2 mile (10 km) run. Of course the same applies to the runner's feet. So individual requirements should be taken into consideration in choosing an appropriate shoe.

That is no easy task. Not every runner knows whether a straight or a curved last is appropriate, whether a heel stabilizer is required, or whether shoes are needed that have features designed to limit pronation or supination.

It is a good idea for someone with a family history of bone or joint injuries who is interested in running to start by getting a basic orthopedic examination. Possible misalignments or incipient injuries to the running mechanism may thus be recognized early and remedied or reduced before they lead to serious consequences (see page 147).

In the examination, the orthopedic doctor can offer important advice on appropriate shoe construction. Those without possible orthopedic— or, for that matter, other potential medical—problems need not consult a physician before taking up running. However, they should seek out a shoe store that specializes in fitting running shoes. Every runner should know and take to heart the deciding factors that come to bear at the point of purchase: the shoe must fit perfectly in terms of length, width, and shape of last.

Shoe Size

The most important consideration in buying shoes is so self-evident that it sounds trite: the shoes have to fit properly!

No problem, right?

Most runners ought to know their correct shoe size (better termed shoe length). However, only about a third of all people have feet of the same length. If you have one foot that is longer than the other, use the longer foot to test shoe size when you are shopping. It should also be noted that in movements such as walking and running, the feet need the extra room provided by another half to a full shoe size. In addition, the feet increase in volume through the course of the day because of heat and circulatory congestion; they are larger at night than in the morning.

Studies on humans have shown that among people who have feet of equal length, only about 40 percent have feet of comparable width. For the rest of the people, the difference averages out to around a half inch (1.3 cm).

If a running shoe is too wide, the foot can move around inside it. That can lead to a number of different complaints. If the runner chooses a narrower shoe that is also shorter (about a quarter inch or 0.6 cm per shoe size), the shorter shoe can produce compression in the toes and even injuries to the arch. On the other hand, as a shoe becomes longer, it also gets wider. For many athletes with small feet, this leads to a serious dilemma.

When necessary, select shoes in different widths from 2A to 4E. Aside from that, the axiom holds true that

trying on the shoes is the best guarantee of satisfactory results. Shop for shoes in the afternoon or evening; wear the shoe in the store as long as possible; run and jump in them; and even bring your own insoles or arch supports as well as the socks that you wear for running.

Uses

The choice of one type of shoe or another also depends on the use to which it will be put. Will the shoe be worn primarily in training or exclusively in competition, mainly for cross-country, in rain and slush, or mainly on the roads? In theory, a *training shoe* should be constructed more sturdily than a shoe used strictly for competition since it will be required to stay in shape for a much greater number of miles.

Racing flats, on the other hand, have little support or motion control but are light and lean and help serious runners cut seconds off their time. Since running shoes are now designed for very specific purposes, select your shoes carefully. Seeking advice from a store that specializes in running shoes or using an online running shoe database is a good idea.

In contrast, most *competition shoes* are constructed strictly with a

A typical women's running shoe:
- *smaller last*
- *lighter weight*
- *greater flexibility*

view to light weight. This is due to the basic, valid observation that additional weight requires higher energy output. Another consideration is that with many runners, the muscles of the foot and lower leg must bring under control improper stresses from functional or anatomic causes. If a very light shoe is worn that provides no support, these muscle groups can be overstressed, and that can lead to premature fatigue and even to injuries. Therefore, for competition over long distances such as marathons, a strong shoe that provides good support is the right choice.

For *cross-country running* on uneven or rough surfaces, a shoe with a relatively broad sole and rough tread is recommended in order to avoid twisting the upper ankle.

Material for the Uppers

Shoes with synthetic fabric uppers are lighter, washable, and breathable (so your feet do not get too hot). To lengthen the shoe's life, wear them only for running and dry them slowly when they are wet. Your running shoe should have a padded tongue to cushion against lace pressure and a padded ankle collar to cushion the ankle and help prevent Achilles tendonitis. Shoes have differently shaped toe boxes that fit different shaped feet. The shoe's lacing system can also be adapted to fit a variety of needs. Use outside holes if your feet are narrow, inside holes if your feet are wide, and avoid the top lace holes if you have high arches. You can also purchase elastic laces that make putting shoes on easy, allow you never to have to tie the shoe, and provide gentle support for the hard-to-fit foot.

Midsoles

One of the most important construction features of a running shoe (and which in recent years has perhaps been the subject of the most intensive research on the part of manufacturers) is the midsole. It provides cushioning, supports the foot, and addresses the needs of all runners with respect to their body weight, leg structure, and running style. The runner's body weight is the simplest consideration. The greater the runner's weight, the harder the midsole should be, and the demands for elasticity and durability are correspondingly greater.

Tipping Inward (Pronation)

It is very important to undergo at least a general analysis of your running style (see "Running Style," page 17). Many runners tend toward pronation, which is often accompanied by landing on the heel. This combination is a natural occurrence. It would surely be wrong to try to explain all types of running injuries in terms of pronation. It is equally wrong to try to fit all runners into shoes with antipronation wedges. There are shoes like that available, but they have a midsole that is harder on the inside toward the rear and softer on the outside. They are appropriate only for runners whose heels tip sharply inward in excessive pronation. Experience shows that pronation supports are required much less frequently than is generally presumed. Most male and female runners are much better served by shoes that have a symmetrically constructed midsole. Further construction features that improve the support qualities of shoes include an inner heel counter that extends far forward and what is known as a heel stabilizer (which nowadays is often incorporated into the midsole). Fairly soft connective tissue allows the arch to sink along its long and broad axes. Oftentimes, changes in leg structure also contribute to knock knees, or overpronation. In such cases, a runner with a view toward finding the qualities described above should choose a strong shoe that has a heel counter and that offers a well-shaped, firm sock liner to support the foot. Individually tailored orthopedic inserts (orthotics), which are prescribed by a podiatrist or a physical therapist, are often desirable to correct biomechanical problems. If you use orthotics, get shoes with sock liners that can be removed and that have enough space to add these custom inserts.

Landing on the Outer Edge of the Foot (Supination)

Many runners, especially ones who land on the middle or the front of the foot and have a tendency to bowed legs (genu varum), have an entirely different set of problems. They face the danger—especially in running over uneven ground—of twisting an ankle. Their soles are worn away on the outside edge, and oftentimes the material used in constructing the uppers fails in the area of the little toe.

The supinator's feet roll outward when running, and they generally have high arches. To see if this is your problem, get your feet wet and walk (do not just stand) on a piece of paper. If you see only the print of your heel and the ball of your foot, your feet probably oversupinate. Your shoes probably show wear on the outsides of the feet, all the way up to the toe. Remember, however, that this is very uncommon. The supinator's feet are more rigid and cannot absorb shock as well as an overpronator's feet, so the supinator is more prone to ankle sprains, stress fractures, and pain on the outside of the shin and knee. Supinators should look for a well-cushioned and flexible shoe.

Neutral Foot Position

In addition to the special cases described above, there are of course a great number of runners whose feet move from a mild supination in landing to a mild pronation in the push off—in other words, perfectly normally. These runners are advised to choose shoes of symmetrical construction (with no special inserts in the midsole either inside or outside). The sole should have good cushioning and guiding qualities in both the forward and rear sections of the foot. For prophylactic reasons, the heel wedge should be fairly low. In my view, only these runners should use a midsole with an air chamber. This type of construction does a fine job of cushioning shock. However, in my experience, it affords little stability for support and footstep guidance in cases where there is a tendency toward harmful lateral stresses.

■ Clothing

Athletic Socks

Properly fitting socks offer the advantages of absorbing a certain amount of sweat and reducing the minor, almost unavoidable slippage that occurs between foot and shoe. In regard to material, we prefer wool or synthetic socks to pure-cotton products since they are more absorbent and they breathe better.

Proper fit is absolutely essential since socks that are too big can rub and bunch up, leading almost without fail to painful blisters. In addition, it is important that there be no seams in the vicinity of the toes; otherwise, they can chafe when you walk or run. Synthetic socks are appropriate for sensitive feet since they prevent rubbing and are capable of absorbing lots of moisture.

There are a wide variety of sock options that fit a variety of needs. Many running socks put additional

"There's no such thing as bad weather . . . "— as long as you are dressed properly.

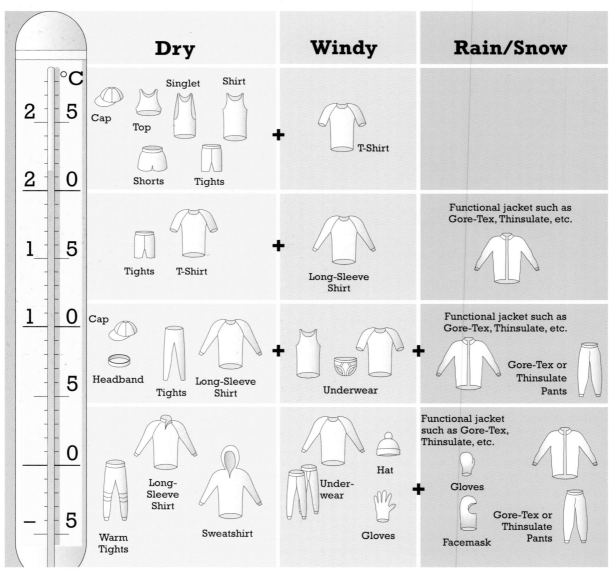

cushioning in strategic places, which implies they provide better support or cushioning. Do not be misled. The purpose of a sock is to keep your shoes clean and to protect your feet from blisters and the elements.

Shorts

A mandatory piece of clothing for all runners is a good pair of running shorts. Nowadays, these come in countless varieties and in high-performance fabrics that far exceed the traditional cotton in regard to durability, ease of care, and hygiene. They are also lighter, dry quickly, and are especially comfortable to wear in the summer. At high and low temperatures, breathable materials made from fibers that do not expand are appropriate (such as polypropylene and similar materials).

Aside from the material, it is a good idea to choose fairly loose-fitting shorts that do not interfere with your stride or squeeze too tightly at the waistband. Built-in undershorts are practical and usually more comfortable to wear than a separate item of underwear. Many shorts are fitted with a practical small pocket where you can keep a handkerchief, your car key, or similar necessities.

Tights

In cool and damp weather, many athletes now prefer to wear tights, tight-fitting long pants made from extremely light and elastic synthetic fabrics. Most of them are a combination of nylon and Lycra, which affords complete freedom of movement. In comparison with traditional warm-up suits, these pants offer the advantage of shedding moisture (rain or sweat) that keeps them from getting heavy and hanging around your legs like a proverbial wet sack. In fact, in light rain they encourage the buildup of a thin insulating layer of moisture on the skin that reduces heat loss and danger of injury.

American female athletes made tights popular in Europe; they have successfully worn them, or even their entire warm-up suits, in sprint competition.

Tights are practical and good looking.

29

Shirts

Materials such as CoolMax have supplanted traditional cotton in the sleeveless running tops known today as singlets. For women, these often rather transparent shirts are available with stripes across the breast and a slightly tighter cut around the neck. When coupled with sports bras, they work for the modest runner in summer.

Warm-up Suit

The warm-up suits that were common a few years ago are no longer worn as much since a light windbreaker and tights are more comfortable to wear. However, a warm-up suit is still useful before and after running.

A warm-up suit in combination with appropriate underclothes is also good in very cold temperatures. The insulating effect depends greatly on the type of material the suit is made from, and the need for conserving heat varies greatly from individual to individual. In addition, many times temperature is not the only determining factor; wind and humidity also come into play. Here is a good rule of thumb: being dressed too warm is better than not warm enough and layers of clothing are the key to warmth.

Additional Clothing

Very cold temperatures, significantly below freezing, make it necessary to wear additional warm clothing to keep from catching cold. Especially in cold weather, colds can hang on for a long time and really drag you down, leading to physical weakness and setbacks in your training. It is essential to keep your torso protected from getting too cold; be sure that your body temperature does not go too low. Warm underwear, perhaps even made from angora wool,

is especially advisable in very cold weather. You can even put on a pair of tights under your warm-up suit in extreme conditions. You also have to keep in mind that you lose lots of warmth through your head and throat; that is why it is a good idea to wear a scarf and a hat. In addition, you have to protect your hands and feet since they can get cold very quickly. The best solution for cold feet is a double layer of thicker socks and a correspondingly larger shoe that leaves room for your toes to move around. We do not yet have truly waterproof running shoes—and running in rubber boots is not much fun at all!

Runners often prefer to wear cotton or wool gloves to keep their hands warm. These afford better temperature control and air circulation than leather gloves do. Mittens, however, are even better than gloves for keeping your hands warm. It is really important to have warm hands when you are running, and really uncomfortable when your hands sweat.

In sum, layered clothing is best in cold weather. No single outfit will suffice. Work with shorts, tights, T-shirts, long-sleeve shirts, and jackets. Mix and match depending on the conditions. Plan to peel off layers as you run. If you are warm when you begin to run, you will be too hot soon enough.

Rain Gear

Most of us have to deal with rain more frequently than with the cold. There are all types of rain gear available on the market. The best of them let the air breathe.

Be sure the seams are covered so that rain cannot sneak in. Aside from purchasing specific gear for rain, you can also apply a spray product, such as Scotch Guard, that helps to make fabrics waterproof. These products

wash off over time in the washing machine. So if you have a great need for rain wear, it may be more prudent to purchase some. A good choice is Gore-Tex.

Gore-Tex is waterproof, but it also lets air and sweat pass through. However, it is very expensive. In cold weather when there is a significant difference between the inner and outer temperatures, Gore-Tex works best, letting sweat out but no rain in. Fairly thin materials that offer a similar function include such brand names as Polartec, Windbloc, and Membrain. The quality of the seams is of paramount importance in how these garments perform.

Reflective vest. For your own safety, wear bright clothing with reflective stripes, a reflective vest, and a "tail-light" at night and whenever visibility is poor.

Training

We can address the topic of training as soon as specific goals are selected. Different runners run for different reasons; therefore, training can mean a number of different things. A recreational athlete may consider a weekly half-hour endurance run to be a significant commitment to training, whereas a competitive runner may put in over 90 miles (150 km) of hard training every week.

The goals and purposes of training vary considerably among individuals, such as participating in citizens' races, competing at higher levels, health maintenance or improvement, or simply improving personal performance.

The contents of a regular, thoughtful training program should depend on the goals you hope to achieve in your running.

A couple of basic rules are generally necessary, though, and of interest to all runners, regardless of their reasons for running.

Training Times

The collective functions of our organism, especially ones that are the products of willful actions, are subject to a synchronized rhythm known as the circadian rhythm. An example of this is the overall hormonal control that fluctuates according to time of day and is expressed in terms of such things as body temperature, appetite, and digestion. In parallel with the periodicity of waking and sleeping, our ability to perform changes considerably in the course of the day, and this varies greatly among individuals. It depends, on the one hand, on an individual's disposition (e.g., there are morning and night people). On the other hand, it is the result of different types of work and lifestyles (e.g., shift work or night work).

Our organism reacts very sensitively to changes in the demands placed on it. I can tell you from personal experience that if you take a flight to another continent such as Asia, you can get used to a totally different time zone within a couple of days. Just the same, I have an uncomfortable memory of the first sleepless nights and the almost unbearable fatigue during the days.

Strenuous training can have a similar effect on our inner clock. At the outset, it may help your body get used to the additional demands of training if you work out at the same time of day whenever possible. That also works best once you become programmed to perform.

Training and Weather

Of course, with our modern lifestyles, it is not always possible to do our workout at the same time every day. Exterior factors such as the weather may also make it advisable to postpone a run.

When it is very hot out, you should try to work out in the early morning or late in the evening in order to avoid health hazards such as sun stroke and heat prostration (see page 144). You should especially avoid very long, intensive runs in the heat of the day. Instead, you can take a 45-minute run of light to medium intensity at most times during the day as long as your fitness level is up to it.

Your body's adaptability to all kinds of weather conditions is improved by regular endurance training as long as the lost electrolytes and fluids are always replaced in adequate amounts. Bad weather is really not a

Autonomous stored reserves

Normal reserves

Physiological performance capacity

Automatic performances

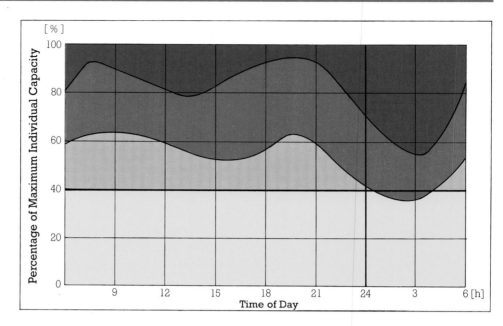

Daytime periodicity of ability to perform; features of performance areas:
1 *Automatic performances that occur without conscious intent (e.g., heartbeat)*
2 *Physiological capacity to perform tasks that require conscious intent without causing fatigue, such as seeing and hearing*
3 *Normal reserves that require a strong intent and that lead to fatigue, such as running*
4 *Autonomous or emergency reserves that cannot be accessed voluntarily*

Circadian rhythm of ACTH and cortisone secretion.

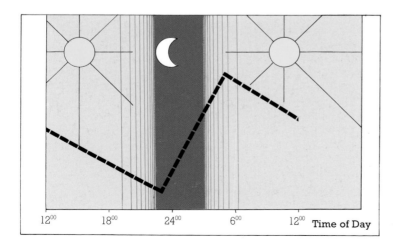

reason to put off training; improper clothing is more commonly at fault. Just the same, rain, cold, and wind can take some of the fun out of running.

On a long run or one that is interrupted by breaks (such as interval training or running hills), you should have some dry clothing along to change into.

Elevated ozone levels should not necessarily be a cause for healthy, fit athletes to cancel a workout. However, fit athletes should try to run before sun up on high-ozone days. In general, it is best to avoid running in ozone if at all possible. Older people, asthmatics, and people who run purely for fitness, on the other hand, should absolutely avoid working out when an ozone alarm is in effect.

Training Facility

Choosing where to train is an important part of setting up a training routine. In many cases, you have to take into account the type of ground you run on, and some types of speed training can best be done only on a track. However, for endurance training, there is no such limitation. Depending on where you live and the type of terrain in your area, you can run on roads, on a track, in the woods, and other places. Some athletes even use the track for part of their long-distance training—an example is Ingrid Kristiansen, the reigning world record holder in the marathon, who works on the track even during the Norwegian winters.

This freedom of course contributes to the fascination with running. What other type of sport offers such minimal demands for equipment and material and can be practiced anywhere so easily?

At this point I would like to discuss the widespread fear that some people have about running on asphalt and similar surfaces. If given a correct running style and good running shoes, a hard, even surface does not involve any heightened risk of injury. On the contrary, since the feet can always be put down cleanly and in a straight line, there is a reduced danger of stress injuries and tendon problems due to twisting. Many top-level athletes like to train on roads since they make it possible to run faster and more safely. (Of course, traffic has to be manageable.) Running in soft sand, on the other hand, is very effective in improving local muscle endurance, strength endurance, and circulatory functions. Over a long time, though, it may interfere with elasticity and impose greater stress on the Achilles tendon. On the basis of many years'

experience, I recommend frequent and regular variations in the places you choose for training.

Physiological Basis for Training

How Training Works

We can explain how training works in the following way:

In response to performance demands (such as training, competition, and even strenuous physical labor), individual cells and the entire body experience what is known as catabolic metabolism (*catabolism*, from the Greek signifying breaking down). That means that by breaking down specific chemical structures, especially carbohydrates and fatty compounds, energy is produced that can be used for such things as running. After the workout is over, the body switches over to the anabolic phase (*anabolism*, from the Greek meaning building up). This restores reserves that have been depleted and prepares the body for the next set of stresses.

If the workload is applied regularly and brought over a certain threshold, it leads to physiological and functional adaptations that affect, respectively, the structure of the body and the ways in which metabolism is carried out. These are what constitute the effect of training, and they are designated by the term overcompensation (see illustration on page 36). Since individual systems adapt at very different rates (e.g., fluid replacement in minutes, carbohydrate regeneration in hours, and protein synthesis in a matter of days to weeks), the illustrated model is merely a gross simplification of very complex and interconnected factors.

35

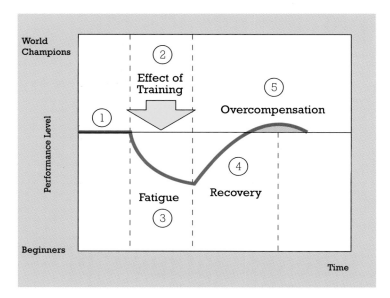

World
Champions

② Effect of
Training

⑤

Overcompensation

①

Performance Level

④

Fatigue   Recovery

③

Beginners

Time

*Theoretical devel-
opment of individ-
ual performance
under conditions of
stress and recovery.*

However, the interplay between
the two programs—stress/activity
on the one hand and rest/recovery
on the other—is not merely the
basis for athletic training. It is the

underlying principle of all life
processes. Unless it is stimulated by
stress and function, every organic
structure atrophies; this is what leads
to muscle shrinkage in a leg that has
been immobilized for three weeks in
a cast. You can easily imagine what
we would look like if we were programmed anabolically, lying in bed
and simply crammed with food, even
for just a couple of weeks.

A knowledge of how metabolism
works will also help us appreciate
that periods of rest and regeneration
are an essential part of training. Only
then can the desired effect be produced. If stresses are applied too frequently or too quickly in succession,
performance drops off unavoidably
after a while since the body is programmed only catabolically and it
does not get a chance to regenerate.
The symptoms include loss of
appetite, sleep disorders, lack of
concentration, weight loss, and other
problems. This is referred to as overtraining.

Adaptation Through Aerobic Endurance Training
(BASED ON J. STIPPIG, A. BERG, AND J. KEUL)

Damping effect of autonomic nervous system	↑
Secretion of stress hormones	↓
Thinning of blood (protection against thrombosis through increased fibrinolytic activity)	↑
Heartbeat	↓
Blood pressure	↓
Oxygen use by heart muscle	↓
Volume of heartbeat	↑
Aerobic capacity	↑
Oxygen absorption in muscle cells	↑
Effectiveness of insulin	↑
Effectiveness of performance hormones	↑
Lactic acid production and excess acidity	↓
Combustion of fatty acids	↑
Cholesterols and triglycerides in blood	↓
Proportion of HDL/LDL fats in blood (protection against arteriosclerosis)	↑

Effects of Endurance Training on Heart and Circulatory System

Whereas strength and speed training
affect only the metabolism of muscle
cells, the body's adaptations to a
varied, structured, and endurance-
based training program include the
heart and circulatory system, autonomous functions, and metabolism.
Changes in the circulatory system are
defined by an increase in aerobic
capacity (*aerobe*, from the Greek
signifying oxygen). In other words,
there is an improvement in the

Key to Chart
↑ = *increases*
↓ = *decreases*

36

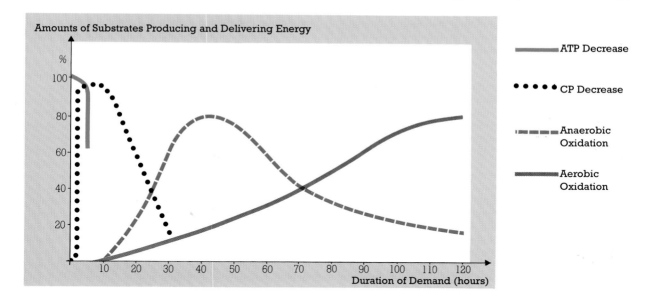

Amounts of Substrates Producing and Delivering Energy

ATP Decrease
CP Decrease
Anaerobic Oxidation
Aerobic Oxidation

Duration of Demand (hours)

relationship between oxygen demand and oxygen availability. Blood pressure diminishes slightly, and heart rate decreases significantly. The heart beats fewer times per minute, requires less energy, and thereby works more efficiently. Since the amount of blood required does not diminish, more blood is pumped through the system with each heartbeat, and the pumping capacity of the heart increases.

The heart muscle becomes stronger. A person who has undergone endurance training always has a greater reserve of energy than a person who has not worked out.

We might draw the following comparison: on the one hand, we have a large-displacement engine in a big limousine that generates its power with low rpms; on the other, the engine from a compact car needs high revolutions to generate power. That also makes it more susceptible to wear and tear.

As capillaries—the smallest blood vessels—are expanded and added, the blood supply to the muscles increases. That makes it possible for the blood to flow more effectively. At rest and under submaximal stress, the autonomic nervous system secretes less catecholamine (known as the stress hormone), which overrides the parasympathetic nervous system.

On the metabolic level, a significant increase in fat combustion equates to an economical use of carbohydrate reserves. Improved insulin effectiveness helps speed the transfer of glucose (blood sugar) from the blood to the cells, where it is used to produce energy. The glycogen reserves in the cells increase, and the mitochondria (sites of energy production in the cells) become larger and more numerous. There are more enzymes available in the respiratory chain to help carry out the chemical processes that deliver energy.

Energy Production for Endurance

Energy requirements for shorter, intensive muscular exertions are based on what is known as anaerobic processes (*anaerobe*, Greek for without oxygen). Among anaerobic mechanisms, we distinguish between lacticidic (involving lactic acid production) and alacticidic (involving no production of lactic acid). Alacticidic

Amounts of different substrates involved in producing and delivering energy. The energy-rich phosphates ATP and CP have the highest flow rate. They are quickly available, but in response to the intensity of the workload, they last a maximum of ten seconds. At the onset of the workload, energy is produced by anaerobic glycolysis, which is adequate for stresses lasting up to a minute. Oxidative processes (aerobic energy production) come increasingly into play. The longer the stress lasts, the more they are used exclusively as an energy source for muscle work.

37

energy production is covered by the energy-rich phosphates (ATP = adenosine triphosphate, CP = creatine phosphate) that are available in the cells. It can support stresses of very short duration up to a maximum of about ten muscle contractions. With greater stresses of 0.3 seconds to 2 minutes, lacticidic energy production dominates, in which glucose is broken down into lactic (milk) acids. For runs at the distances of 1,312 to 2,250 feet (400 to 800 m), this is the most important source of energy, just as it is for a burst of speed in longer runs. High levels of lactic acid produce excessive acidification in the muscles and the entire body, which may force the person to cease the activity. Speed and strength training develop this type of energy production almost exclusively, as do certain games such as squash, tennis, and volleyball.

As the duration of the stress increases—and this of course involves a simultaneous decrease in the intensity of the stress (that is, stride cadence)—energy is produced more and more by aerobic means. In other

words, by using oxygen, glucose and fatty acids are broken down into the metabolic products CO_2 (carbon dioxide) and H_2O (water). Since this does not lead to accumulation of by-products, the stress can be sustained for a very long time. The term steady state refers to a balance between energy use and energy production. Lactic acid levels can be kept constant. This is not possible, though, beyond the maximum lactic acid steady state. In reality this is synonymous with what we refer to as the aerobic-anaerobic threshold. The stress becomes too intense and contributes to increased lactic acid levels. This acidity is a cause for discontinuing the stress or at least for reducing it significantly.

Relative maximal oxygen absorption has been established as a measure of organic performance capacity among endurance-trained athletes. This is influenced by the size of practically the entire heart and circulatory system and the amount of materials needed for energy metabolism.

This is the amount of oxygen per minute, keyed to body weight, that

Amounts of aerobic and anaerobic capacity in energy production at maximum stress of differing duration: the duration of the stress and an example of how that is transferred to corresponding distances are indicated logarithmically on the abscissa. It can be seen that with stress that lasts over two minutes, aerobic metabolism is the primary energy source. With stress of short duration, especially types of stress that correspond to a 330-foot or 656-foot (100-m or 200-m) run or primarily require the use of strength, the majority of the required energy is provided anoxidatively, whether through breakdown of available energy-rich phosphate reserves or through glucolysis. The calculations apply to people with high aerobic and anaerobic capacity.

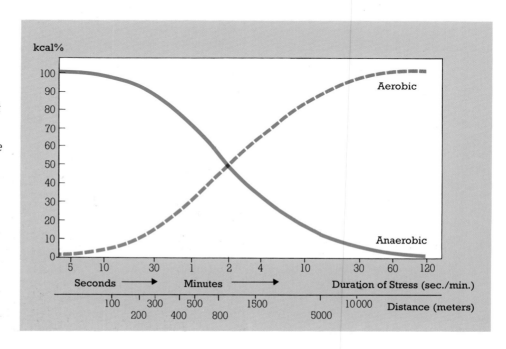

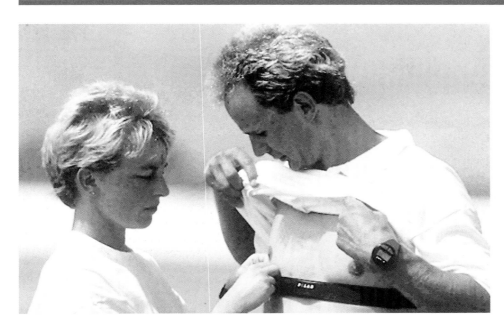

Heart rate monitors offer the best possibility for precise control of intensity during a workout.

an athlete can take into the blood through the lungs and utilize in the muscle cells at a maximum level of stress. The higher the capacity for maximum oxygen intake, the longer submaximal levels of stress can postpone utilizing the "costly" energy that is produced anaerobically. This means that lactic acid buildup is bound to set in sooner or later at higher speeds.

With people who are not in shape, the maximum oxygen intake is about 737 cubic inches (45 ml) per minute and 2.2 pounds (1 kg) of body weight. With recreational athletes, it's about 984 cubic inches (60 ml) per minute and 2.2 pounds (1 kg). Top-level athletes (such as Henry Rono from Kenya when he was at his peak) can reach an astonishing level of 1,393 cubic inches (85 ml) and more.

Monitoring Heart Rate

Measuring heart rate (pulse) is the most reliable and therefore trouble-free option for checking the

Computer-assisted evaluation of heart rate measurements.

functioning of our heart and circulatory system.

In conjunction with individual testing, this constitutes an objective control over training intensity as a prerequisite for an effective training program. A heart monitor is recommended for measuring the pulse precisely. It records the action of the heart and effects a wireless transmission of information to a receiver about the size of a wristwatch. Either EKG electrodes or a chest belt is used to take the measurements. The receiver on the wrist displays your current heartbeat in various ways depending on the model. It also stores the values in intervals of up to five seconds (with 3,000 storage areas in all), records intermediate times, and inputs upper and lower pulse limits. When these are crossed, an acoustic signal sounds. After

running, you can call up the values manually or transfer them by interfacing with a computer.

■ Types of Training

Long-distance Running

Long-distance running is the basic form of any training program for running. It serves to build up the organism's capacities (such as improving aerobic capacity) that enable the runner to undertake the intensive training that targets competition. This involves a run of fairly long duration at an even cadence. In that context, three rough categories can be identified.

It is very important to control the intensity of the workload in long-distance running. The effect on the body of a relaxed, moderate run of about 45 minutes and an all-out marathon run are understandably very different.

In connection with running speed (or intensity of workload) different types of training can be identified. As long as energy is produced under conditions of adequate available oxygen, the body experiences no buildup of lactic acid. The lactic acid level remains at 2 mmol/l or lower. Long-distance runs at this slow pace are referred to using the term pure endurance 1 (PE 1).

If the speed is increased, the result is a minor increase in lactic acid, which reaches a level between 2 and 4 mmol/l; this can be maintained at a steady level for quite a while. This type of training is known as a mixture of aerobic and anaerobic activity (PE 2).

At higher running speeds, the lactic acid level is forced over the aerobic-anaerobic threshold. In spite of an even cadence, the lactic acid level continues to increase, until acid buildup forces cessation of the activity or at least a significant decease in speed. Very fast workouts of that type are referred to using the term *speed endurance*.

Unfortunately, individual control over speed usually is not accomplished by feel, as many experienced runners have found out. Feel depends on a great number of factors, such as our outlook on life, career orientation (A-type personalities usually go too fast!), climate and weather, overall atmosphere, how the runner feels on a given day, and so forth.

Oftentimes, an individual in a group will unwittingly be stimulated and manipulated to adjust to the other runners. In a group of ten runners, usually only one or two are running at the right speed; all the others are going too fast, or more rarely, too slow.

Determining the level of lactic acid at specific running speeds is a reliable indication of the type of training going on. The relationship involving lactic acid level, heart rate, and running speed produces a current, individual fingerprint of a runner's performance ability. There is a heart rate that corresponds to every lactic acid level and that can be easily controlled by using a heart rate monitor.

Admittedly, that is a comparatively expensive option, but it is helpful and reliable in regulating the intensity of endurance training.

Distance Running with a Regenerative Component

The cadence should be low enough to produce a workload below the threshold (i.e., lactic acid is less than 2 mmol/l). The purpose of this kind of run involves stimulating the circulatory system and metabolism either to prepare the body for a future increase in workload (e.g., before competition) or in order to stimulate the recovery mechanisms after strenuous exertion (active recovery). An experienced runner cannot expect any major training benefit from a single run of this type. However, in the overall structure of training, relaxed, fairly long endurance runs still form a necessary and valid basis, and should always amount to 25–75 percent of the week's activity.

The situation is different for beginners, whose training should at first consist primarily of relaxed distance running. This relaxed endurance run can be broken up into different segments that are interspersed with walking breaks or calisthenics. This will amount to a long-distance run composed of intervals as a temporary solution on the way to running for 30 to 40 minutes without a break.

Individually Tailored Distance Run

Fitness, age, the season, the weather, how the runner feels, and many other factors make up what we call the training standard of the endurance athlete.

The cadence should be high enough and the distance long enough to produce an adequate training effect. The duration of this type of run should not be less than 40 minutes. The best training tempo is determined most accurately by measuring lactic acid. Alternatively, beginners can achieve acceptable results by several simple means:

1. Talk to each other!

As you run, if you are able to maintain a conversation with your partner(s), the cadence is not too high. This observation is based on:

2. The Correlation Between Breaths and Strides

That is, four steps per breath (in other words, breathing in for four steps and breathing out for four steps) to stay within the realm of aerobic training. If you can take only three steps per breath, you are functioning inside the aerobic-anaerobic realm. If you can take only two steps per breath, your running speed is over the aerobic-anaerobic threshold.

3. The Conconi Test

Professor Conconi from Ferrara, Italy, has developed a testing procedure that avoids the need to draw blood. The method is based on the fact that as running speed increases, heart rate (pulse) increases along a straight line. When the aerobic-anaerobic threshold is reached, the rise in heart rate flattens out. That makes it possible to deduce the individual's lactic acid level and type of training.

Personal experience has shown that the Conconi test is most useful when it is applied to the same person numerous times under identical conditions (what is known as a longitudinal section). A test that is done just once may involve a fairly high margin of error since a person first has to learn how to do the test. Usually, the test is conducted on a treadmill (in which case there should be plenty of fresh air available) or as a field test on a track.

An audible signal elicits a gradual increase in running speed (e.g., 3.5 mph (6 km/h), 4 / mph (7km/h), and 4 fl mph (8 km/h) for 656-foot (200 m) intervals). For reliable test results, at least ten levels of workload should be reached.

Tempo Runs

This type of training is appropriate only for competitive runners. The cadence should be set at a level that can be maintained for 15 to 20 minutes. That means that the runner is training above the aerobic-anaerobic threshold.

Speed endurance runs are very good preparation for road runs and are used worldwide by nearly all the good marathon runners. The purpose of the workout is to maintain an even, high speed, faster than competition tempo, over a shorter course.

Speed Play ("Fartlek")

The name means "playing with different running speeds." These variations of endurance runs were made popular by Scandinavian runners (hence the name fartlek), but nowadays they occupy a solid place in the training regimens of athletes throughout the world. They involve more variety than the usual distance runs, and they are very effective at the same time.

Yobes Ondieki from Kenya, the first human to run 6.2 miles (10 km) under 27 minutes, pictured here practicing a speed endurance run.

Sample Speed Play Workouts

Type of Training	Training Goal	Guidelines
Speed play (pyramid shaped)	Aerobic and anaerobic endurance	10 min. warm-up run 2 min.*—(2 min.)— 3 min.*—(3 min.)— 4 min.*—(4 min.)— 6 min.*—(6 min.)— 4 min.*—(4 min.)— 3 min.*—(3 min.)— 2 min.*—(2 min.)— 10-min. cool-down run
Speed play (minute runs)	Aerobic and anaerobic endurance	e.g., 10-min. warm-up 10 × 1 min.*—(1 min.)— 10 min. cool-down run

Items designated with * are to be done at quicker speed endurance tempo, those in parentheses at a slower endurance cadence.

"Swedish" Speed Play

In this basic form of speed play, the runner adjusts running speed to the conditions of the terrain. Understandably, moderately hilly routes in woods and fields are preferable to straight and level roads. Some stretches are run quickly, and others are done at a slower pace. The overall run is similar in effect to an endurance run.

"Polish" Speed Play

In this case, adjustments keyed to terrain are replaced by variations dictated by time. That makes this type of training usable on roads and on terrain that does not offer much variety. After a warm-up phase, faster and slower stretches are run in accordance with a preestablished plan. The distances may be of varying or equal length. The latter case is analogous

Types of Hill Training

Type of Workout	Training Goal	Guidelines
Hill runs (extensive interval method)	Anaerobic and aerobic endurance, local muscular endurance, strength endurance	e.g., 15 hilly laps, each with 200 m easy climb and 400 m gentle downhill, without break, emphasis on climbing; 10-minute warm-up and cool-down runs
Hill runs (intensive interval method)	Anaerobic and aerobic endurance, local muscular endurance, strength endurance	e.g., ten 400 m climbs, breaks of 2 to 2-1/2 min., jog back; 15 min. warm-up and calisthenics and cool-down runs
Hill runs (repeat method)	Anaerobic endurance, local muscular endurance, strength endurance	e.g., 5 × 500 m climbs (almost top speed), breaks of six to ten minutes; walk back to start; 30 min. warm-up including runs for form and speed, 20 min. cool-down run

Left: Hill training in threes some years ago.

Below: The same trio running the hills today—ten years later at the same place (still crazy after all these years).

Training

S = Set
BS = Break between sets
SR = Speed run

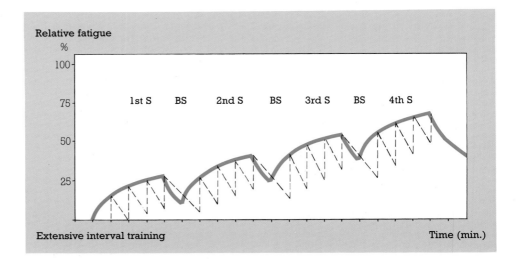

Relative fatigue
%

1st S   BS   2nd S   BS   3rd S   BS   4th S

Extensive interval training   Time (min.)

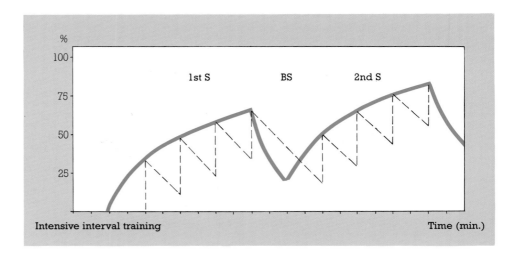

%

1st S   BS   2nd S

Intensive interval training   Time (min.)

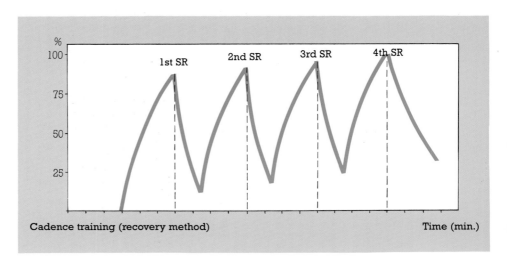

%

1st SR   2nd SR   3rd SR   4th SR

Cadence training (recovery method)   Time (min.)

Training methods for improving anaerobic endurance.

to extensive interval training integrated into an endurance run.

Mountain Training (Hill Running)

Many athletes appreciate this type of training as an alternative to training on the roads. It makes it possible to carry out fairly high-intensity training in the countryside and have an effect on various physiological and variable dimensions. Depending on age, fitness, season, and training goal, hill training can be done in accordance with extensive or intensive interval training or the repeat method. All types of training place demands on the circulatory system. Simultaneously, there are major demands placed onto local muscular endurance in the legs, where lactic acid buildup increases in proportion to the workload selected. Additionally, hill training contributes to strength endurance.

While the first two examples in the chart at the bottom of page 44 are appropriate for endurance athletes who sometimes take part in local road races and hill runs,

repetitive hill running is generally a good choice only for well-prepared, competitive athletes. This consideration places the hill running primarily in the second preparation phase, in spring and early summer. General training in the winter can also be spiced up with interval-type hill-running workouts. Occasional hill running on the repeat principle will accomplish the same thing during the competitive season.

Interval and Speed Training

Training on a track makes sense for everyone, although athletes who wish to take part in track meets will find it especially useful. This type of training, like hill training and circuit training for developing strength, can be divided into three main groups: extensive interval training, intensive interval training, and speed training based on the repeat principle.

Extensive Interval Training

This is understood to mean a type of training that involves alternating intensive and more relaxed segments. The intensity and duration

Sample Track Workouts Based on the Extensive Interval Method

Type of Training	Training Goal	Guidelines
Track workout (extensive interval training)	Aerobic and anaerobic endurance	e.g., for a 5,000 m runner with a personal best of 15:00 min.: 15 × 400 m, ⌀ 70 sec.; rest with 1 to 1-1/2 min. jogging; 15 to 20 min. warm-up and cool-down runs
Track workout (extensive interval training)	Aerobic and anaerobic endurance	e.g., for a woman 10,000 m runner or marathoner with personal bests of 40:00 min. and 3 hrs. 20 min., respectively: 10–15 × 600 m, ⌀ 2:15 min., rest with 2 to 3 min. jogging; 15 to 20 min. warm-up and cool-down runs

47

Sample Track Workouts Based on the Intensive Interval Method

Type of Training	Training Goal	Guidelines
Track workout (intensive interval training)	Aerobic and anaerobic endurance	e.g., for a 5,000 m runner with a personal best of 15:00 min.: 6 × 800 m, ∅ 2:20 min., rest with about 4 min. jogging; 20 min. warm-up and cool-down runs
Track workout (intensive interval training)	Aerobic and anaerobic endurance	e.g., for a woman 10,000 m runner or marathoner with personal bests of 40:00 min. and 3 hrs. 20 min., respectively: 6 × 800 m, ∅ approx. 3:00 min.; rest with approx. 4 min. jogging; 20 min. warm-up and cool-down runs

of the workload are chosen in such a way that they can be repeated often and after only short pauses of jogging. The purpose of this type of training is to run faster than at competition cadence and, at the same time, to get in an extensive workout. In that regard, this workout is comparable to speed play. Lactic acid buildup is only moderate. This amounts to a mixed type of training where improvement in aerobic and anaerobic qualities are targeted. This type of training can be conducted in various ways practically throughout the entire year.

Intensive Interval Training

The goal of this similarly composite type of training is largely an increase in anaerobic capacity. In other words, it will achieve a greater buildup of lactic acid than with extensive interval training.

Running speed is higher in the individual segments, and the rest breaks between sets are longer. For many long-distance runners, this constitutes the most intensive form of track workout and is used as a type of preparation for competition. The separation between extensive interval

Sample Track Workouts Based on the Repeat Method

Type of Training	Training Goal	Guidelines
Track workout (repeat method)	Anaerobic endurance	e.g., for a 5,000 m runner with a personal best of 15:00 min.: 3 × 1,000 m, approx. 2:42 to 2:45 min., rest breaks of 6 to 10 min. walking/jogging; 30 min. warm-up incl. work on form and speed, 20 min. cool-down runs
Track workout (repeat method)	Anaerobic endurance	e.g., for a woman 10,000 m runner or marathoner with personal bests of 40:00 min. and 3 hrs. 20 min., respectively: 3 × 1,000 m, approx. 3:30 to 3:40 min., rest 6 to 10 min. walking/jogging; 30 min. warm-up incl. work on form and speed, 20 min., cool-down runs

training on the one hand and speed training based on the repeat principle on the other are fluid, depending on how they are done.

Speed Training Based on the Repeat Principle

This is a type of training for competitive athletes that is used primarily for track runners and only briefly in peak season. The athlete strives to achieve maximum lactic acid buildup. The shorter the distance, the greater the value of this type of training for the athlete. Middle-distance runners (800 m and 1,500 m) train more frequently and more intensively with this method than long-distance runners do (5,000 m and longer). It addresses mainly the anaerobic energy-producing processes.

Workouts usually consist of a few runs of medium distance at high to very high speed. The length of the rest breaks does not have much effect on the results.

Planning and Periodizing Training

As already explained, the effect of training on the human body involves adjustment to repeated workload stimuli. For adults, this means that performance can be expected to improve only if there is a parallel increase in training. In order to bring about continuous improvement and avoid excessive strain and health-threatening injuries, it is a good idea to plan your training regimen very carefully.

Training Log

For every plan, an initial requirement is a current statement of position. In other words, your starting point consists of such things as the extent of your training (miles/kilometers run per week), training frequency (number of workouts per week), training intensity (e.g., speed endurance in minutes per mile/kilometer), and perhaps even competition results.

For this purpose, you should maintain a training diary in which you record all this information plus perhaps a few brief notes on how you feel, body weight, weather conditions, and so forth. This type of information is very helpful if at some point you want to compare the goals you identified for yourself and the results you have actually achieved (see page 74 for detailed instructions).

As you plan your training, it is useful to identify short, medium, and long time periods.

Long-term Periodizing (Macrocycle)

The longer the time period on which a training plan is based, the less flexible it is. It cannot take into account fluctuations in form or improvements in performance. Long-term plans that cover several years may serve as a framework that helps orient a runner in preparing for a particular competition (such as the Olympic Games) or achieving some personal accomplishment.

If you are a beginner, for example, and have begun training by setting a goal of running a marathon in under four hours, you should work up to it over several years by using the guidelines in the graduated development training plan on page 51.

Model for developing form in a year-long cycle with periodizing involving one and two peaks.

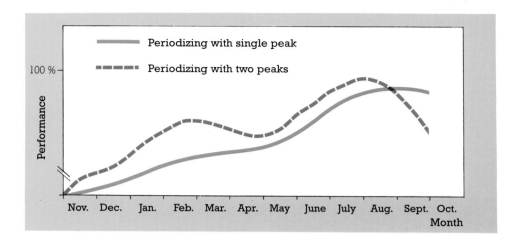

Medium-term Periodizing (Mesocycle)

Within medium-term periodizing (usually one year), the tasks for the coming 12 months are identified with respect to the training that has taken place up to that point. A relevant example is the training plan of a long-distance runner who takes part in track competitions during the summer and who wants to peak during that time.

Sample Workouts for One Week in Preparation Period I (Six Workouts)

Type of Training	Training Goals	Guidelines	Frequency per week
Distance run	Aerobic endurance	Approx. 1 hr., relaxed to medium speed; finish with stretching	Three times
Speed Play	Aerobic and anaerobic endurance	e.g., 30–40 min. core program; 10 min. warm-up and cool-down runs	Once
or:			
Training on track (extensive interval method)— best used in second half of preparation period I	Aerobic and anaerobic endurance	Moderate speed (e.g., 1,000 m race speed), moderate distance (e.g., 500–1,000 m), fairly short rest breaks; 15 min. warm-up, incremental, and cool-down runs	Once
Circuit training (1 set jumping exercises, 1 set general strengthening exercises)	General strength and endurance	Mostly after extensive interval method, e.g., 45 min. core program, 15 to 20 min. warm-up and cool-down runs	Twice

Sample Workouts for One Week in Preparation Period II (Six Workouts)

Type of Workout	Training Goals	Guidelines	Frequency per week
Endurance	Aerobic endurance	Approx. 1 hr. medium speed	Three times
Hill running (extensive interval method)	Aerobic and anaerobic endurance, local muscle endurance, and strength endurance	e.g., 10 laps over hilly 800 m course including approx. 300 m uphill and 500 m downhill (emphasis on climb); 10 min. warm-up and cool-down runs	Once
Hill running (intensive interval method)	Anaerobic and aerobic endurance, local muscle endurance, strength endurance	e.g., 8 × 400 m uphill, trot back (= 2–3 min. break), 15 to 20 min. warm-up and cool-down runs	Once
Circuit training	General strength and endurance	Intensive interval or control method; e.g., 45 min. core program, ample running for warm-up and cool-down	Once

Preparation Period I

Preparation Period I (November to February) serves primarily to improve basic fitness. It is built around training measures with a high endurance component (distance runs, speed play, and extensive interval training). At the same time, general strength and strength endurance should be increased by means of regular circuit training.

Mary Decker-Slaney, shown in the lead, was the dominant woman middle-distance runner in the early eighties. Brigitte Kraus (no. 150) has held the German record for the 3,000-meter run for over ten years.

**Sample Workouts for One Week in Competition Period I
(Five Workouts)**

Type of Workout	Training Goals	Guidelines	Frequency per week
Endurance	Aerobic endurance	Approx. 45 min. medium speed	Twice
Speed play	Aerobic and anaerobic endurance	e.g., 20 to 30 min. core program; 10 min. warm-up and cool-down runs	Once
Track workout (extensive interval training)	Anaerobic and aerobic endurance	e.g., total distance of 5 to 7 km, speed higher than 1,000 m race speed; jogging breaks, 10 min. warm-up and run for form; 10 to 15 min. cool-down run	Once
Track workout (intensive interval training)	Anaerobic (and aerobic) endurance	e.g., total distance of 4 to 6 km, fairly high speed and longer breaks, as with ext. interval training; 10 min. warm-up, 15 min. coordination exercises; 15 min. cool-down run	Once

Preparation Period II

In Preparation Period II (March through April), the emphasis is shifted slightly. The endurance component remains in place, but strength endurance is fostered through regular hill training in special and particular ways. At the same time, anaerobic metabolism is developed.

Competition Period I

Competition Period I (May through June) ushers in the competitive season; this is when fairly easy competitions should begin (also consult "Competition," page 105). Naturally, it is a good idea to prepare for these with appropriate workouts on the track. The general scope of training can be reduced slightly.

Competition Period II

Competition Period II (July through September) involves entering more competitions. This is when you should reach your peak conditioning. The scope of your training and the importance of aerobic endurance in training are cut back (but keep GA 1 over 25 percent!). Very specific training measures that directly target preparation for competition come to the forefront.

Recovery Periods

These very arduous weeks conclude with a regeneration phase (September through October). This provides recovery and preparation for training in the coming winter.

*Page 53:
Irish runner Sonia
O'Sullivan (no.
495) dominated
the 3,000- and
5,000-meter runs
in the nineties.*

Short-term Periodizing (Microcycle)

The detailed planning of every workout is done in accordance with short-term periodizing. Short-term information and influences are built into training in three- to four-week cycles. Many athletes prefer to increase the scope and intensity of their training in a rhythm where a week of fairly hard work is always followed by a week of recovery. Others prefer the workload to increase slowly over the entire training period.

Of course, this type of program does not become the Gospel just because it is written down. You do not have to follow it whether the sun shines or a hurricane rages. The more experienced the athlete, the more likely it is that information of a subjective nature (how the person feels, fitness, health, workload, and so forth) and objective information (e.g., weather, light conditions, condition of the terrain used for training) are incorporated into the conceived plan to constitute a harmonious training program.

Working closely with a personal trainer can also be extremely helpful in this case.

Sample Workouts for One Week in Competition Period II (Four Workouts)

Type of Training	Training Goals	Guidelines	Frequency per week
Endurance run	Aerobic endurance	Approx. 40 min. at an easy pace	Twice
Speed play	Aerobic and anaerobic endurance	e.g., 20 to 25 min. core program with intensive efforts and fairly long jogging breaks; also 10 min. warm-up and cool-down runs	Once
or:			
Track workout (intensive interval training)	Aerobic and anaerobic endurance	e.g., 5 to 8 repetitions at fairly high speed, 3 to 4 min. breaks; 25 min. warm-up and coordination development; 15 min. cool-down run	Once
Track workout (Speed runs on repeat principle)	Anaerobic endurance	e.g., 3 to 4 repetitions at very high speed over distances from 600 to 2,000 m; long rest breaks; 25 min. warm-up and co-ordination development; 15 min. cool-down run	Once
or:			
Speed endurance run (control run)	Aerobic and anaerobic endurance; when used regularly, this helps verify conditioning	e.g., total distance of 4 to 6 km, fairly high speed and longer breaks, as with ext. interval training; 10 min. warm-up, 15 min. coordination exercises; 15 min. cool-down run	Once

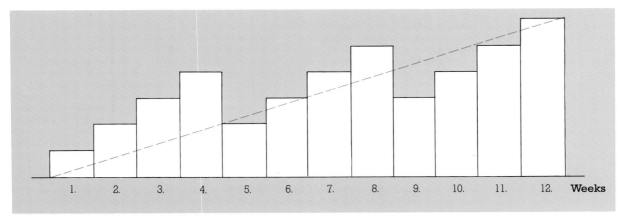

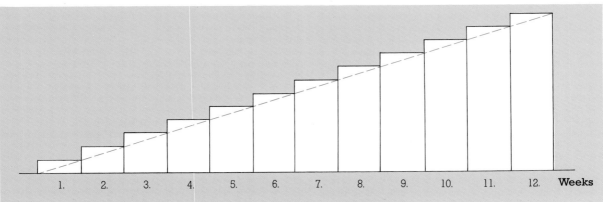

Training for Children and Youth

We continually read about so-called wonder kids who turn in amazing times in marathons. Supposedly that is no major problem for the children since when they play, they put in long distances, seemingly without tiring. It is true that children can move around for hours without experiencing fatigue. However, precise observation shows that this type of movement is not regular and continuous. Rather, it is interrupted by frequent breaks and is more like intervals. The reason for that is the reduced aerobic capacity of the child's body, which up to the tenth year of life is subject to only

moderate endurance training—a type of self-protection for the young body against overtaxing the heart and circulatory system.

Added to that is the aversion that children have to regular, monotonous types of activity. It is much more in line with their nature to seek variety and continually changing stimuli. Parents, teachers, and coaches should keep that in mind when they encounter either aversion to or talent for running in children.

Training for Children (Up to About the Age of 14)

Up to the age of about 14 (that is, the end of pubescence, the first phase of maturation) the main

Stepped (above) and regular (below) increases in training load within a training period.

Running is great fun for children too, but they should exercise caution in moving up to longer distances.

However, if anything is neglected early on, in many cases it cannot be made up for later. The results may be a lack of speed and poor running style.

Injuries are often the result of faulty technique or insufficient physical conditioning; this applies to running as well as to most other types of sports.

Up to the age of 14, growing children should become familiar with the following types of training and goals:
- ☐ General, broad-based instruction in basic exercises
- ☐ Learning simple gymnastics exercises
- ☐ Broad training in basic track-and-field skills (jumping, running, and throwing)
- ☐ Easy types of circuit training
- ☐ As many different types of sports as possible for the sake of variety

This is particularly important in improving the strength of children and youngsters. Strength is an effective factor in preventing injuries due to faulty posture and a prerequisite for developing other motor skills.

Training for Youngsters (Starting Around Age 14)

In adolescence, during the second phase of the maturing process (starting around the age of 14) some specific endurance and strength training can begin gradually. That, of course, depends on physical development since endurance training that is begun too early can often lead to psychological burnout in young people before they reach their peak performance. Only very few junior national champions at middle and

consideration in training should be varied and basic development, especially an improvement in flexibility (suppleness), coordination (cooperation between the central nervous system and the musculoskeletal system for a specific type of movement), overall strength, and speed. These basic motor skills can be developed with no danger to body or spirit even at an early age, as long as they are presented in a playful, varied program.

Another consideration is that children and youths are very quick learners in these areas and pick up complex movements a good deal faster and more thoroughly than adults do.

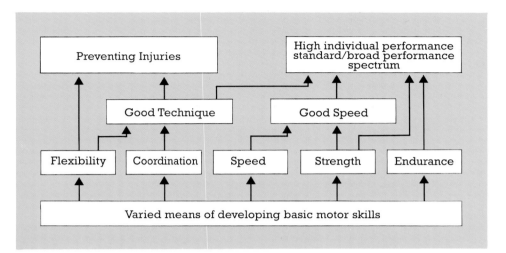

```
┌──────────────────────┐          ┌──────────────────────────────┐
│  Preventing Injuries  │          │ High individual performance   │
│                      │          │ standard/broad performance    │
└──────────────────────┘          │         spectrum              │
                                   └──────────────────────────────┘

          ┌──────────────────┐          ┌──────────────────┐
          │  Good Technique   │          │    Good Speed     │
          └──────────────────┘          └──────────────────┘

┌───────────┐ ┌──────────────┐ ┌──────────┐ ┌──────────┐ ┌──────────┐
│Flexibility │ │ Coordination  │ │  Speed    │ │ Strength  │ │ Endurance │
└───────────┘ └──────────────┘ └──────────┘ └──────────┘ └──────────┘

┌────────────────────────────────────────────────────────────────────┐
│        Varied means of developing basic motor skills                 │
└────────────────────────────────────────────────────────────────────┘
```

Developing the main types of motor skills in children and early adolescents.

Regular training for running should be used as the primary type of training for youths only after adolescence.

Types of Workouts for Middle- to Long-distance Runners
Training Plan 1 (Up to Age 12)

Type of Workout	Training Goals	Guidelines	Frequency per week
All-around exercises/ circuit training	Flexibility, speed, general strength, and endurance	Use intensive interval method or control method	Once
Technique training	Learning complex motions/coordination	Cold months: basic training in gymnastics on apparatus Warm months: track disciplines, e.g., practice starts, hurdles, jumping, throwing	Once
Ball games	Overall strength and endurance, coordination, speed endurance	Basketball, handball, soccer, volleyball	Once

Training Plan 2 (Ages 12 to 14)

Type of Workout	Training Goals	Guidelines	Frequency per week
Variety of running	Speed, coordination	10–15 min. warm-up run, emphasis on sprinting, developing reactions/starts, running technique	Once
At first: all-around physical training/circuit training	Flexibility, speed, general strength and endurance	Use intensive interval method or control method	Once
Technique training	Learning complex movements/coordination	Varied warm-up program (warm-up run, exercises for stretching and flexibility, perhaps ball games or other games involving running); General and special technique development in - track-and-field disciplines with running, jumping, and throwing	Once
Varied Training Runs	Coordination, speed	10–15 min. warm-up run, development runs, practice starts, jumping exercises, functional exercises	Once
At first: ball games	Overall strength and endurance, coordination, speed endurance	Basketball, handball, soccer, volleyball	

Training Plan 3 (Ages 15 to 17 or 18)

Type of Training	Training Goals	Guidelines	Frequency per week
Assorted training runs	Speed, speed endurance, stamina	15–20 min. warm-up run emphasis on sprinting, short intervals, or speed runs	Once
Followed by all-around exercises/circuit training	General strength and endurance	Use intensive interval method or control method	
Technique training	Learning and perfecting complex movements	15–20 min. varied warm-up program with particular emphasis on individual preferences/talents	Once
Varied training runs	Coordination	15–20 min. warm-up run, running instruction, practice jumping;	Once
Followed by ball games	Overall strength and endurance, coordination, speed endurance	Basketball, handball, soccer, volleyball	
Long-distance run	Endurance (aerobic)	30–40 min. at relaxed speed; perhaps end up with ball games	Once

Training Plan 4 (Over Age 17 or 18)
Summer Months

Type of Workout	Training Goals	Guidelines	Frequency per week
Intensive interval training	Endurance (anaerobic and aerobic)	15–20 min. warm-up program; coordination runs, intensive interval training, plenty of running to cool down	Twice
Long-distance run	Endurance (aerobic)	30–50 min. stretching and step-ups after most runs	2–3 times
Up to May: circuit training	Overall strength and endurance	Intensive interval method, control method	Once

Winter Months

Type of Training	Training Goals	Guidelines	Frequency per week
Circuit training/ general physical conditioning program	Overall strength and endurance	15–20 min. warm-up run; extensive/intensive interval method; cool-down run or ball game	Once
Strength training	Various types of strength (maximum output, speed strength, strength endurance)	15–20 min. warm-up program, stretching exercises Extensive/intensive interval method, end with runs of increasing intensity	Once
Extensive interval training	Endurance (aerobic and anaerobic)	15 min. warm-up run, coordination runs, cool-down run	Once
Long-distance run followed by stretching	Endurance (aerobic flexibility)	40–60 min. relaxed-to-medium speed	2–3 times

long distances break through to become a national or international presence as adult men and women runners. That should be a cause for reflection. In my opinion, this is why it can be a disadvantage to specialize too early.

How to make running fun!
Running as a group experience is
of tremendous value to many
recreational athletes.

Training Advice for Fitness Runners

In this section, I turn my attention to the growing group of runners to whom numbers and times are of no consequence. For them, running is a means of healing or keeping their bodies healthy. They seek a natural antidote to the monotonous, often heavy psychological demands they experience in their work. The significance of regular physical activity has been proven in many countries,

especially in the United States. In many businesses and enterprises, sports of all types have been advanced at the demand of and with the participation of business leaders. In Europe, there are associations and business athletic clubs that offer opportunities and equipment (including facilities, changing rooms, and coaching) for getting together with like-minded people in an instructional setting.

In the United States, many corporations have running teams that participate in corporate cups. While some of the teams are quite competitive, others are developed for corporate team building and support.

Beginners can develop their running by first walking the distance they wish to run and then, over time, including running breaks in their walks.

The next step in training is to cover the entire distance without walking breaks. However, you need to be flexible in meeting your self-imposed goals. We are not machines. Our physical constitution is subject to many influences and continually fluctuates to different degrees among individuals. So go ahead and take a break if you need to. Stretch out and relax your arms and legs, and pay more attention to your body's "voice" than to your ambition. Let the other people calmly pass you by if they are more up to it on a particular day.

The best training frequency for fitness runners is three to four times a week at about 40 minutes per run. Slow running is not necessarily better than fast running from a health standpoint, but duration is the most important factor. Therefore, run at a pace that will allow you to run for the prescribed time. Take your pulse regularly. You will find more detailed information on this on page 39.

A similar training effect can be achieved in other sports as well, as long as they involve dynamic movement and major muscle masses are brought into play. Very worthwhile sports besides running include the type where the workload has a more beneficial effect on the autonomic nervous system, game-type sports are less effective.

Go ahead and change the type of sport any time you have the desire and an opportunity. Fun and health are closely connected to one another. You should not neglect to do some exercises and stretching, you need to provide a balanced and varied workload for your body. Remember: in case of doubt, slow down!

Training Principles for Fitness Runners

☐ Build up gradually to the best workout frequency.

☐ Keep track of your individual target heart rate.

☐ Stick to dynamic types of sports that place continual demands on the circulatory system.

☐ This should be fun!

Training Advice for Recreational Runners

The advice in the preceding section also fully applies to recreational race participants. With appropriate preparation and training, fitness runners can also take part in competition if they wish to. A difference here is that training for these people becomes competition-oriented and keyed to their motivation and fitness level. This gives the performance factor greater importance in planning and developing a training program.

The basic rules of training apply to all athletes. It is just that there are

Training Principles for Recreational Racers

☐ Organic basis

☐ Basic preparation for competition

☐ Age-appropriate training methods

☐ Overall fitness

some significant differences with regard to the effectiveness of individual types of training.

Organic Basis

For every long-distance runner, it is of primary importance to strengthen the heart and circulatory systems (GA 1 and GA 2).

Aerobic metabolism is the most important performance factor for all runners over distances exceeding 1,500 meters. It is also responsible for a quick recovery after experiencing a workload, and it provides the need for fairly intensive interval training.

Basic Preparation for Competition

Stamina, i.e., anaerobic endurance, is the second important performance factor. As already explained, this is even more important at shorter race distances. This means that if you intend to take part only in races over 6 miles (10 km) long, you do not have to do any training on a track. It would be better for you to try to reach your peak by doing appropriate workouts on roads and trails. This includes hill running, speed play, and speed endurance runs (see page 40). Just before important competitions, you should cut down on the scope and intensity of your training.

Age-Appropriate Training Methods

Selecting the right type of training involves, in addition to setting goals, one more factor that needs to be taken into consideration: the runner's age. Even though the human body can still benefit from endurance training into the seventies, the body's adaptability to anaerobic workloads continually decreases starting about the end of the third decade of life. The main reason for this is changes in muscular structure, which does not

Even in the "best years of their lives," people can expect to make good progress by training—as long as they have a little patience.

stop or reverse even in response to hard speed training. This fact should be taken into consideration in planning individual training. In my opinion, repeats on a track for a midfifties runner are inappropriate.

Even if running is the cream of all types of sports for you, you should practice some complementary types of sports as a way to protect your body from injuries. It is especially important to do some types of circuit training to increase overall strength and some regular stretching to preserve a full range of movement in all joints (see pages 77 and 86). Remember that endurance training requires a lot of patience. It takes quite a while for the body to respond to the heightened workload. You have to give it time and increase your training dosage in small increments—a maximum of 18.6 to 24.8 miles (30 to 40 km) per week over a year's time.

The "Grand Prix" in Bern, Switzerland owes a lot to the incomparable atmosphere of the Old Town.

64

Sample Workouts for a 40-Year-Old Recreational Racer

This runner takes part in competitions between 6.2 and 15.5 miles (10 and 25 km) in length, trains an average of four times per week, and

Build-up Phase (Winter months)

Type of Workout	Training Goals	Guidelines	Frequency per week
Distance run	Aerobic endurance	Approx. 10 km medium speed; end with 15 min. stretching	Once
Distance run	Aerobic endurance	Approx. 15–20 km, easy speed; end with a bath or a swim	Once
Speed play, individually structured (Swedish)	Aerobic and anaerobic endurance	Approx. 12–15 km amounting to total workload of approx. 15–20 min.; finish work with 15 min. stretching	Once
or: Hill runs by extensive or intensive interval method	General aerobic and anaerobic endurance, local muscle endurance	Uphill efforts of 300 – 600 m, downhill jog to recover; warm-up and cool-down runs including stretching exercises	Once
Circuit training	General strength and endurance	15 min. warm-up, e.g., using extensive interval method, fairly long workloads with brief breaks; 30 min. easy cool-down run	Once

Competition Phase

Type of Workout	Training Goals	Guidelines	Frequency per week
Distance run	Aerobic endurance	10–12 km easy-to-medium speed; end with 15 min. stretching and step-ups	Twice
Speed play	Aerobic and anaerobic endurance	Total of individual segments 10–15 min., finish with stretching	Once
Speed endurance	Anaerobic and aerobic endurance	15–20 min. at about 10 km race speed; 15 min. warm-up cool-down runs; finish with stretching	Once

puts in about 24.8 to 37.2 miles (40 to 60 km) in training.

Sample Workouts of World-class Athletes

There are numerous factors that affect progress in performance at top levels of international track competition. Such things surely include acceleration (increasing speed of development and average size of people in developed nations) and improved material and technical conditions (such as shoes and running surfaces). In my view, though, progress for advanced runners comes from the type of training they do. Based on scientific knowledge about training and the physiology of performance, people are training on a more intensive and broad basis than ever before. No one seems to know for

sure where the limits lie. The only sure thing is that today's top-level athletes are operating at the edge of what is physically and psychologically manageable. Because runners have to negotiate a type of tightrope walk between too much and too little training, preparation for a running season often takes on the aspect of a game of chance. Not all influences can be understood exactly. Even minor shifts in a person's health can upset the delicate state of balance. By way of information, we include the training program from some world-class athletes. The following examples will at least confirm that the age-old maxim still applies: no pain, no gain.

If we were to compare the training methods of various top-level athletes classified on the basis of performance, we would find agreement on the underlying principles but some noticeable differences among individuals. Every runner has a particular program that is keyed to personal strengths and weaknesses, preferences and dislikes, climate, and circumstances. For that reason, you cannot become another Sebastian

*Page 66:
A qualifying heat including distance runner Dieter Baumann.*

Grete Waitz (November 1981) Basic Training

	First Workout	Second Workout
Monday	11 km medium-endurance run: 43 min.	Approx. 4 km warm-up run 6 × 1,000 m in 3:10–3:15 min. (1-1/2 min. break) on park grounds, approx. 4 km cool-down run
Tuesday	13 km medium-endurance run	Approx. 5 km easy-endurance run followed by mild strength training
Wednesday	11 km medium-endurance run	Approx. 4 km warm-up run 8 × 500 m (1-1/2 min. break) on park grounds; approx. 5 km cool-down run
Thursday	13 km medium-distance run	Medium-endurance run
Friday	11 km medium-endurance run	Approx. 5 km warm-up run, 15 × 100 m coordination runs, approx. 5 km cool-down run
Saturday	11 km very comfortable endurance run	
Sunday	11 km endurance run	13 km medium-endurance run

Grete Waitz of Norway won the New York Marathon seven times between 1978 and 1985 and for years was the world's record holder in the marathon.

Grete Waitz (January 1985) Preparation for Road Running

	First Workout	Second Workout
Monday	10 km medium-endurance run	10 km medium-endurance run
Tuesday	13 km medium-endurance run	
Wednesday	4 km warm-up run 3 sets 3 × 300 m (each set run easy, medium, and hard) 5 km cool-down run	6.5 km relaxed-endurance run
Thursday	11 km easy-endurance run	
Friday	10 km medium-endurance run	
Saturday	5 km warm-up run 10 km road run 32:44 min. cool-down run	
Sunday	14.5 km very easy-endurance run	

Thomas Wessinghage (March 1982) Preparation Period II

	First Workout	Second Workout
Monday	11.4 km endurance run, 41:50 min., including 5 × 150 m hill runs; in between, 150 m jogging breaks; stretching	10 km speed play: 33:51 min. (warm-up run, 10 × 1 min. fast/ 1 min. slow, cool-down run) stretching, jumping exercises, runs of increasing intensity
Tuesday	11.4 km endurance run, 40:37 min., including 5 × 150 m hill runs (in between: 150 m jogging breaks); stretching, jumping exercises, runs of increasing intensity	10 km speed play: 32:51 min. (warm-up run, 9 × 1/2 min. fast/ 2 min. slow) stretching, jumping exercises, runs of increasing intensity
Wednesday	11 km endurance run, 40:27 min., including 5 × 150 m hill runs (in between: 150 m jogging breaks); stretching, jumping exercises, runs of increasing intensity	3.5 km warm-up run 10 × 300 km; 43 sec. (2 min. jogging break) jumping exercises, 3.5 km cool-down run
Thursday	4 km warm-up run, stretching, step-ups 3 × 200 m: 5:36 min.(in between, 5 min. jogging break), 4 km cool-down run	
Friday	10 km speed play: 33:02 min. (warm-up run, 8 × 1 min. fast/ 2 min. slow); stretching	11.4 km endurance run: 39:29 min., including 5 × 150 m hill runs (in between, 150 m jogging, stretching, jumping exercises, runs of increasing intensity
Saturday	8 km relaxed-endurance run: 30:00 min.; stretching, jumping exercises	4.5 km warm-up run 12 × 120 hill climbs and stairs 4.5 km cool-down run
Sunday	13 km relaxed-endurance run 50:00 min.; stretching, jumping exercises, runs of increasing intensity	

Thomas Wessinghage (August 1982) Competition Period II

	First Workout	Second Workout
Monday	9.5 km endurance run, 32:00 min., stretching runs of increasing intensity	4.5 km warm-up run stretching, step-ups 2 × 600 m: 82 sec., 1 × 300 m: 38 sec. (95 min. jogging break for each); 5 km cool-down run
Tuesday	15 km endurance run, 53:20 min.	15 km endurance run: 53:45 min.; stretching, step-ups
Wednesday	9.5 km relaxed-endurance run, 35:10 min.; stretching, runs of increasing intensity	4.5 km warm-up run stretching, step-ups 3 × 200 m: 24.5 sec. (4-1/2 min. break for each) 5 km cool-down run
Thursday	15 km relaxed-endurance run: 57:00 min.; stretching, runs of increasing intensity, jumping exercises	
Friday	15 km endurance run: 55:30 min.; stretching, runs of increasing intensity	4.5 km warm-up run stretching, step-ups 3 × 300 m: 37.5 sec. (4 min. jogging break) 5 min. cool-down run
Saturday	14.5 km relaxed-endurance run: 52:30 min. relaxation exercises	
Sunday	10 km easy-endurance run 37:15 min.; stretching, jumping exercises, runs of increasing intensity	9.5 km endurance run: 33:40 min. stretching, step-ups

In addition to the great events such as the Olympics and the World Championships, international meets (such as the ASV Sports Fest in Cologne) still have the greatest attraction for athletes and spectators.

69

Coe simply by copying his training regimen, which in itself is impossible.

Alberto Cova Competition Phase

During the last phase of the preparation period for the 1986 European Championship in Stuttgart, where Alberto Cova started in the 10,000 m (second) and 5,000 m (finalist), he got in five track workouts in the following 15 days. They included two to three days of only easy-distance runs, stretching, and active regeneration measures. Cova's trainer, Giorgio Rondelli, believes that the basic concept of training is fairly consistent among the current world's best long-distance runners.

Certain minor differences exist in quantity and quality of individual programs.

Alberto Cova (right; on the left, Gianni de Madonna) was the most successful 1,000 m runner in the early eighties. He won the 1982 European Championship in Athens, the 1983 Helsinki World Championship, and was the winner at the 1984 Los Angeles Olympics. That was the last time Western runners dominated at this distance.

First workout	20 × 400 m; average 60 sec. (50 sec. break for each)
Second workout	2 × 3,000 m: approx. 8:06 min. (8 sec. break for each); end up with 3 × 1,500 m: approx. 3:58 min. (6 min. break for each)
Third workout	6 × 1,000 m: approx. 2:30 min. (5 min. break for each)
Fourth workout	1 × 800 m: 1:57 min. (3 min. break) 4 × 200 m: approx. 27 sec. each (30 sec. break for each) 1 × 1,000 m: approx. 2:30 min. (5 min. break) 4 × 300 m; approx. 43 sec. each (30 sec. break for each) 1 × 600 m: approx. 87 sec. (5 min. break) 4 × 200 m: approx. 27 sec. each (30 sec. break for each)
Fifth workout	1 × 2,000 m: 5:14 min., last 800 m in 1:57 min. (8 min. break) 1 × 1,500 m: 3:50 min., last 800 m in 71 sec. (8 min. break) 2 × 800 m: 1:56 min. each, last 300 m in 40 sec. (8 min. break)

In 1995, the Cuban runner Anna Fidelia Quirot (no. 252) returned to her old form after a serious accident.

Altitude Training

For generations, people have taken advantage of the stimulating qualities of the climate in high-altitude regions.

Endurance athletes such as runners, rowers, cyclists, and cross-country skiers have also long been aware of the performance-enhancing effect of high-altitude residence. Medical opinion does not overlap seamlessly with the experiences of athletes, so perhaps a part of the high-altitude effect is attributable to psychological effects. However, every year many of the world's best athletes can be found in the foremost high-altitude training centers. The most famous ones include St. Moritz and Davos in Switzerland, Font Romeu in France, Boulder, Colorado and Flagstaff, Arizona in the United States, and Eldoret in Kenya. Earlier, this list also included Mexico City.

The human body is forced to undergo adaptive measures at altitudes over a 3,100 feet (1,000 m) above sea level. These are brought about primarily by the lack of oxygen in such places. This condition first becomes evident in breathing, the heart and circulatory system, and the blood. With fairly long residence at a level between approximately 4,650 to 6,820 feet (1,500 to 2,000 m) above sea level, which is ideal for training, you can expect to experience noticeable altitude adjustments after about three weeks.

The adaptation process passes through two stages. The body gets enough oxygen despite lower levels in the atmosphere because the breathing, the heart and circulatory system, and the blood are actively stimulated. It is especially significant that more red blood corpuscles are produced. In addition, the cells change the way they work producing

Adjustment Effects on the Body due to Altitude-Induced Lack of Oxygen (Based on Barbashova)

On the organic level:
- ☐ Increased number of red blood cells
- ☐ Stronger breathing
- ☐ Enhanced circulation
- ☐ Changes in acid-base balance in the blood
- ☐ Changed blood enzyme activity

On the cellular level:
- ☐ Increase in myoglobin
- ☐ Changes in cell enzyme activity
- ☐ Improved oxygen utilization
- ☐ Reduced oxygen consumption
- ☐ Increase in anaerobic energy production
- ☐ Increased resistance of cells to oxygen depletion

more energy anaerobically, without using oxygen from the air.

For runners, this means that merely staying at high altitudes has a mild training effect. Workouts done at high altitudes have a greater effect than ones done at low altitudes. Runners have to keep this in mind to avoid the very real danger of overtraining. Therefore, it is not advisable to use the accustomed training program without changing its scope and intensity when moving to a higher altitude. For the first three days after arrival, you should take it easy and avoid training very strenuously. Often people experience a euphoria produced by a fairly significant hormonal reaction. This results in elevated circulatory and oxygen exchange levels that can conceal the true amount of strain. Do not let that lead you astray. If you start to increase the scope of your training gradually, the following clues may be of use; they have been condensed from the experience of numerous athletes over the course of several years.

☐ Average endurance speed in comparison with low-land training should be reduced. From time to time, you can throw in a brisk endurance run, but not until a week has gone by.

☐ In interval training, rest breaks should be longer, and perhaps even the number of repetitions should be reduced. Shorter runs up to about 1,640 feet (500 m) can then be done at about the same intensity as at lower altitudes. On the other hand, longer runs should be done at a lower speed.

I would like to stress once again that this is based on individual experiences. They should not necessarily take precedence over yours.

Altitude training is still in the experimental stages. Some training groups are trying such things as "sleeping high, training low." They train in lower areas in order to keep the workload at a high level of intensity. It is known that there is a greater strain in the first three days and on the seventh or eighth day. In addition, when athletes stay at high altitudes, they sometimes have to cope with mild sleep disturbances.

Appetite and thirst increase, and the danger of infection is greater at a high altitude. Therefore, it is important to eat and drink enough. It is also a good idea to take supplementary vitamins (especially vitamin C) and iron.

Another important question for athletes involves setting the date for the first competition after altitude training. There is a variety of opinions on this topic.

My experiences indicate that you should not compete on the first or second day after coming down from a high-altitude training area. Rather, you should train lightly for the first three days in the low land. After that, you can throw in a fairly easy trial. You also have to keep in mind that after a week or ten days, you may experience a decline in performance. Therefore, I would plan to do a particularly important race within two weeks of returning from altitude training. Of course, the performance-enhancing effects of staying at a high altitude do not last forever. However, you can assume that positive effects will still be felt after about four to six weeks, even if they are merely psychological in nature—and this is not said in any pejorative sense.

Training Diary

Practically all world- and national-class athletes keep a training diary. The reasons they do this apply also to enthusiasts at lower levels who likewise may want to take part in competition.

Regular notations allow the runner to accomplish personal bests and compete successfully as well as understand failures. The keys and lessons that come out of this may help reduce mistakes in the future and foster successful training measures in a more regular and purposeful way. As they prepare for important races, many athletes return to proven programs that have helped achieve good competition results in the past.

The attached chart that I used makes it possible to get an overview of the training in several categories and provides a quick orientation. Both sides of one page are enough to record the notes for a month's training.

The first column is designed as a running calendar in which you can write in the days of the week. Next to that you find six tiny columns for recording the subjective level of difficulty or the effort you expended in the individual workouts. The scale goes from 1 (very easy) to 6 (very strenuous). At the same time, you can use different colors in the same chart to identify the goal addressed by any workout. The following six categories can be used:

Blue: Endurance training (distance run, aerobic workload)

Purple: Stamina (interval training, hill runs, speed play, and anaerobic workload)

Red: Speed (sprint training, step-ups, and coordination training)

Yellow: Active recovery (regenerative endurance run, swimming, etc.)

Green: Strength and overall conditioning (strength training, circuit training, complementary sports, and exercises)

Black: Competition

For example, an easy distance run would be indicated in blue on difficulty three; a difficult interval workout could be marked in purple on level 5. In addition, the average heart rate under workload can be recorded and put to good use.

There is also room in this training diary for additional information. The daily and weekly mileage or kilometer counts can be recorded in different areas. You can record time and place of training plus external conditions such as temperature, rain, sun, wind, and so forth.

There is another column where you can record how you feel, including any illnesses, injuries, or other individual factors that affect training. The columns for pulse rate at rest and body weight serve a similar purpose. Resting pulse should be taken under comparable conditions—always early in the morning, right after you wake up and before you get out of bed. Also weigh yourself in the morning, on an empty stomach. Since you are looking for net weight, weigh yourself in the nude. Usually the beam balances that you find in hospitals and doctor's offices are more reliable than common spring-type bathroom scales.

Month **May**

Day	Exertion						km		Place/Time	Training—Terrain, Type, Breaks—Training
	1	2	3	4	5	6	Day	Wk.		
Tues. 1			■				10		New York, 6:00 P.M.	Level park ground, easy distance run
Wed. 2				■			13		New York, 4:00 P.M.	Warm-up/cool-down runs 8 km, 5 × 1,000 m
Thurs. 3	■						8		Philadelphia, 4:00 P.M.	Easy regenerative distance run, 8 km, 38 min.
Fri. 4		■					12		Mecherude, 4:30 P.M.	Easy distance run, 12 km, exercises, step-ups
5										
6										

On the last page of the training diary there is room to record details of competitions. A yearly survey of the training diary makes it possible to draw up a curve of the distances run every week and your average body weight. In addition, the number of workouts per week—keyed to the previously described categories of endurance, stamina, speed, active recovery, strength/general conditioning, and competition—can be noted. You can also identify stages where you experienced illnesses or injuries.

The most important information of interest to athletes who train regularly is thus documented in a way that is useful and easy to review.

Year's Overview

Week	1	2	3	4	5	6	7	8	9	10	11	12	13	14
Kilometers Run 130														
120														
110	X	X												
100	X	X												
90														
80														
70														
Endurance	4	5	4	3										
Stamina	2	-	1	-										
Speed	-	-	1	1										
Recovery	1	-	1	-										
Conditioning	-	2	-	-										
Competition	-	-	-	1										
Body Weight in kilograms 72														
71														
70	X			X										
69		X	X											
68														
Illness				X										
Injury														
Menstruation														

Below: Sample training diary

	Active Pulse Rate	Weather	Weight	Passive Pulse Rate	Health (Illnesses, Injuries)
	142	Sunny, mild	70	46	Healthy
	183	Sunny, mild	69	45	Healthy
	130	Mild, windy	69	46	Fatigue
	144	Overcast	70	46	Healthy

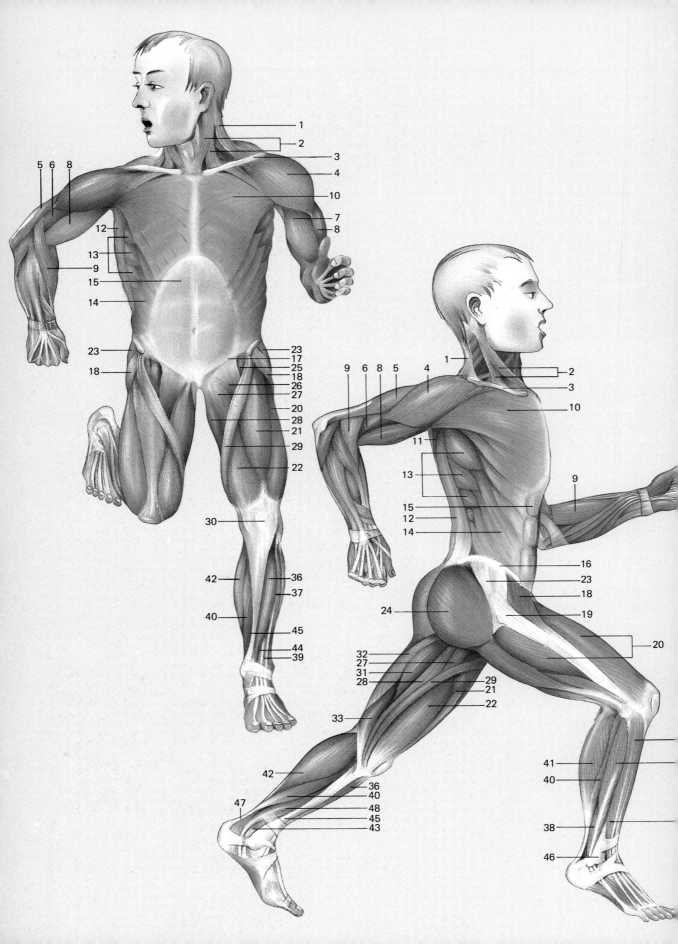

Physical Conditioning

There is a saying to the effect that "Running is the only way to learn how to run." It is trite, but it does reflect some important ground rules about training. However, it is also important to consider that "It takes more than running to learn how to run fast!"

All of today's top-level athletes train using very complex programs that include not only elements related to running but also various tangential training measures. These help eliminate particular weaknesses and foster strengths. They also play an important preventive role; they help avoid injuries that may occur through heavy doses of one-sided training. The types of experiences that top-level athletes have can also help fitness runners and other running enthusiasts. The measures described in this chapter focus on the athlete's musculature—whether it needs stretching, strengthening, better coordination, or relaxation. The drawings on page 76 should provide a fairly easy, if superficial, orientation to what the runner's musculature

looks like in action, without the protection or interference of skin and a sheath of subcutaneous fat.

Stretching

Nowadays, the training program of every runner must include stretching and relaxation exercises for the muscles. Regular stretching is essential to every top-level athlete. Even casual and fitness runners should do a program of exercises several times every week. Training places our skeleton and muscles under workload, and only a proper stimulation from training can produce the desired effect. Unvarying types of workload can lead to a shortening of the muscles. The improper stresses and alternative movements that involves can produce strain on other structures such as tendons, ligaments, and neighboring muscle groups.

Stretching serves to return the muscles to their normal tone and prevent injuries. It should also be noted that everyone is endowed by nature with different degrees of flexibility. That means that it does not make much sense to judge your flexibility by the standards of female gymnasts. It is much better to try to

1. M. trapezius	10. M. pectoralis major	19. Tractus iliotibialis	33. M. semimembranosus	42. M. gastrocnemius, caput mediale
2. M. sternocleidomastoideus	11. M. teres major	20. M. vastus lateralis	34. M. biceps femoris, caput longum	43. M. tibialis posterior
3. Clavicula = collar bone or clavicle	12. M. latissimus dorsi	21. M. rectus femoris	35. M. biceps femoris, caput breve	44. M. extensor hallucis longus
4. M. deltoideus	13. M. serratus anterior	22. M. vastus medialis	36. M. tibialis anterior	45. Tibia = shinbone
5. M. triceps brachii	14. M. obliquus externus abdominis	23. M. gluteus medius	37. M. peroneus longus	46. Fibula = shinbone/ outer ankle bone
6. M. brachialis	15. M. rectus abdominis	24. M. gluteus maximus	38. M. peroneus brevis	47. Tendo calcaneus = Achilles tendon
7. M. biceps brachii, caput breve (short head)	16. Crista iliaca = crest of ilium	25. M. iliopsoas	39. M. extensor digitorum longus	48. M. flexor digitorum longus
8. M. biceps brachii, caput longum (long head)	17. Ligamentum inguinale = inguinal ligament	26. M. pectineus	40. M. soleus	
9. M. brachioradialis	18. M. tensor fasciae latae	27. M. adductor longus	41. M. gastrocnemius, caput laterale	
		28. M. gracilis		
		29. M. sartorius		
		30. Patella = kneecap		
		31. M. adductor magnus		
		32. M. semitendinosus		

improve or at least maintain your flexibility through a sensible, regular, stretching routine that is done properly. Consequently, you should warm up with an easy jog or distance run of about ten minutes' duration before you pitch into your regular program.

When we talk about stretching, it is useful to distinguish between dynamic stretching (stretching exercises) and static stretching. The forceful bobbing and pulling motions that were common some time ago are wrong. They can lead to muscle tears and strains and may even reduce flexibility. Short, very forceful stretching movements activate the reflex curve of the muscles.

Stretching the axis of the muscles leads to a contraction of the same muscles, and that interferes with maximal stretching. Excessive tensing of muscles that are stressed in that way can even lead to injuries. In practice, a combination of dynamic and static stretching exercises has proven to be effective.

Dynamic Stretching

The four exercises illustrated here simply provide a selection that can be complemented with a few more exercises of your choosing. They are intended to help loosen up and relax the muscles. Immediately at the end of the warm-up or distance run, use the possibility of active recovery to calm down your breathing and circulation before doing real stretching. When these are done properly, they also help develop coordination and activate the muscles through speed and strength exercises (such as bounding). You should be especially relaxed when you do them; they need to be gentle, not abrupt.

Sample Exercises

① **Parallel Arm Swings**
Feet are about shoulder width apart and pointed slightly outward. With the upper body erect and arms held high, let your arms fall gently to the front; keep the spinal column from

① *Parallel arm swings*

② *Torso twists*

bending too far to the rear. Breathe out forcefully, and swing your arms far to the rear as you lightly flex your knees. Use your spinal erector muscles to apply light tension to your back and keep the spinal column relaxed and straight. A rounded back or "wood chopper's stance" would place significant strain on the lower back, perhaps even damaging intervertebral disks. Breathe in again as you raise your arms.

② Torso Twists
Feet are about shoulder width apart and pointed slightly outward. Arms are held horizontal and are swung first to the right, then to the left; the upper body, shoulders, and head turn with them.

This stretches the shoulder and torso muscles and makes the spine more flexible.

③ Side Bends
Feet are about shoulder width apart and parallel. Arms are clasped behind the head and the body is bent to one side. The torso should not be twisted. This stretches the muscles on the side of the torso and the shoulder muscles and contributes to flexibility of the spine in the lower back and chest areas.

④ Opposing Arm Swings
Use the same starting stance as with exercise number one; upper body and head are held erect. Both arms are swung in opposite directions next to the body, far to the front and the rear. Keep some tension in the upper body, and bounce slightly in the knees.

③ *Side bends*

④ *Opposing arm swings*

Stretching Through Antagonistic Tensing and Relaxing

The hamstring or ischiocrural muscu-lature is an example where active stretching by means of tensing and relaxing is appropriate (for illustra-tion of this antagonistic stretching, see page 85). As you lie on your back, raise one leg vertically as you bend the hip at a right angle. The opposing leg is straightened and pressed against the ground; toes are stretched upward. This position actively stretches the bent knee up to the point where you can feel the tension in the hamstring muscle (but not so much that it becomes painful!). Release after a few sec-onds by flexing the knee, and then actively stretch again. Do about ten repetitions, and keep increasing the stretch in the hamstring muscle.

Static Stretching

Static exercises make up the real heart of the stretching program. The following selection involves all the important muscles in the body for runners. You should stretch slowly and continuously, without bouncing or bending, for about 20 seconds per repetition on each side of the body. Above all, you should avoid doing these exercises too forcefully. The tension you feel at first should diminish the longer you do these exercises, and they should never be painful. Your breathing should be easy, even, and relaxed and never forced. Just as with yoga, correct performance of these stretching exercises produces a harmonious physical and spiritual relaxation. That is another good reason why stretching has become an important

part of the training and competition-oriented warm-up program of so many top-level international athletes.

Sample Exercises

① Lower Leg and Calf Muscles (M. Gastrocnemius)

In a striding stance, place your hands at shoulder height on a wall, fence, or something similar. Feet are kept parallel. The forward knee is bent and the rear one is straightened to form a straight line from the shoulders down to the heel. The body is lowered as much as possible without raising the rear heel from the floor.

② Lower Leg (M. Soleus)

By using the same starting position as in the previous exercise, the rear foot is about one foot's length closer to the front. The bottom is thrust slightly rearward, and the rear knee is bent as much as possible.

③ Lower Leg and Front Shin Muscle (M. Tibialis Anterior)

While kneeling, your bottom is gradually lowered onto the heels. This produces stretching in the shin muscle on the side of the anterior tibial muscle (m. tibialis anterior). You may wish to place a small cushion under your bottom or your ankles.

④ Thigh Muscles (M. Quadriceps)

As you stand on one foot, bend the stretching leg as much as possible at the knee and pull it by hand toward your bottom. The hip joint is completely stretched, and the pelvis and spine are stabilized by tensing the stomach muscles. Bend the knee of the support leg slightly. This stretching affects the four-fold thigh muscle (m. quadriceps), especially the m. rectus femoris. This is an important measure in avoiding knee problems (i.e., chondropathia patellae/kneecap cartilage disease).

⑤ This same exercise can be done even more efficiently as you lie face down. This permits ideal stretching in the hip. While you do the exercise, keep the pelvis pressed firmly against the ground. Stretching is accomplished by actively bending the knee.

⑥ Upper Leg and Hamstring Muscles (Ischiocrural Musculature)

The important stretching of the muscles that bend the knee is done in a standing position. The support leg is slightly bent, and the leg being stretched is advanced a half step. By tensing the spinal erectors, the lower spine is locked to the pelvis so that by inclining the upper body forward (while maintaining the lumbar lordosis or hollow in the back), the pelvis is tipped to the front. The back of the thigh is stretched, and the spine and the disks are protected by the corset of muscles (see also how this exercise is done lying down on page 160, number 3).

⑦ Inside of Upper Leg (Adductors/M. Gracilis)

Start with feet spread, one knee bent, and the other straight. The torso is slowly and deliberately bent over the arm resting on the hip and in the direction of the straightened leg. The other arm is held over the head and is used in stretching the side. This exercise mostly stretches the adductors (m. gracilis) on the inside of the thigh. This muscle is

important in stabilizing the pelvis when you are running over uneven ground, and it helps in running at high speed.

⑧ Groin Area and Hip Muscles (M. Iliopsoas)

Get into a lunging position, and use one hand to support your upper body. By slowly pushing the pelvis to the front, you stretch the iliopsoas (stomach-loins-leg muscles). Caution: to reduce pressure on the menisci of the forward bent knee, the lunging position should reach far forward and form a right angle of the knee.

⑨ Bottom Muscles (M. Gluteus Medius/Minimus)

As you lie on your back, bend one leg at the knee and hip, and use the opposite arm to pull it toward the middle of your body. The arm on the same side is extended for support. Keep the back as flat as possible against the floor so it does not twist.

⑩ Shoulders and Large Chest Muscles (M. Pectoralis Major)

Runners may experience problems with the vertebrae in the neck and chest area. Stretching exercises are effective in combating rounded shoulders, which can be produced by a shortened large chest muscle. Raise one arm above horizontal, and hold a tree, post, door frame, or something comparable. Stretch by turning head and torso. At the same time, the muscles around the shoulder blades should be tensed.

Example of Postisometric Stretching

Stretching the Adductors

In a sitting position, place the soles of the feet together and the feet relatively far in front of the body. The hands grasp the ankles, and the elbows are supported on the knees. Now try for about five seconds to move the knees together against the resistance from your elbows.

Between exertions, the upper arms slowly and continuously push the knees away from each other a little at a time, without bouncing.

This puts you into a new starting position with your legs spread farther apart; repeat the process from this position.

This method of stretching is very effective but not entirely carefree, so use it with caution. Any time you feel discomfort, you should stop doing the exercise. Not all muscle groups can be stretched in this way without the help of another person. The partner must proceed with extreme caution, though, and never attempt to overcome muscle resistance by using force.

Postisometric stretching for the inner thighs (adductors).

*Intermittent
stretching*

Intermittent Stretching

Although people used to frown upon any stretching movements done during static stretching, several studies have recently shown that even dynamic stretching or repeated tensing and relaxing of individual muscles or muscle groups can greatly improve elasticity. This "intermittent stretching" can be compared to agonistic-antagonistic stretching (see page 80). This also has to do with the neuromuscular laws of the muscles. Gentle, soft movements are important in doing these stretches.

85

■ Strength Training

The amount of strength needed for endurance is comparatively small. Performance in endurance sports involves primarily performance in circulatory and metabolic functions. Just the same, a good level of strength is essential even for endurance athletes. It is both for optimizing performance (since greater strength translates into improved economy in running and greater performance reserves) and especially for preventing injuries (by reducing faulty movements and improper stresses).

Training effects are always specific. For muscles, this means that strength is not improved by endurance training but only through stimuli that require a much higher muscular tension.

Strength training involves the necessary workload stimuli and thereby stimulates the muscles to adapt (with an increase in strength and possibly in size).

Representation of two motor units.

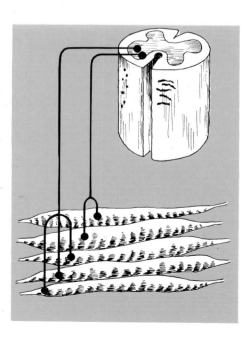

Physiological Basis

The proportion of muscles in the overall weight of the human body is about 25 to 30 percent in women and 40 to 50 percent in men.

Individual skeletal muscles consist of a quantity of muscle fibers, which in turn are made up of hundreds of muscle fibrils. Inside these fibrils, the protein structures produce actin and myosin, the contractile elements; these enable the muscles to contract. The order for this contraction or shortening is issued in the motor centers of the cerebral cortex, the brain stem, and the cerebellum. It is transmitted through what is known as the pyramid route of the spinal cord and the motor nerves at the muscles. The individual nerve fibers and the muscle fibers that it supplies are designated by the term *motor unit*.

There are three types of muscle fiber: quick fibers (which are white), slow fibers (red), and an intermediate type. Quick fibers are capable of contracting more rapidly than the slow fibers, but as a result, they tire sooner. They are responsible for fast, strong movements and get their energy primarily from anaerobic metabolic processes. The slow fibers, on the other hand, are available for tasks that require endurance and are well supplied with energy produced aerobically. The properties of the intermediate-type fibers place them between the two previous ones.

All three types of fibers are always present in muscles but in differing proportions. This seems to be a factor controlled by heredity. In other words, the physiological qualities of the muscles in what we recognize as talent are determined by genetics. The type of demands placed on the muscles make it possible to change the proportions of muscle fibers to a certain degree. It is probably the intermediate-type fibers that are capable of being transformed in one direction or another. Since the relative portion of slow muscle fibers increases as we grow older, it seems that in principle it should be fairly easy for a good sprinter to turn into a decent distance runner rather than the opposite.

Types of Strength

Strength interacts closely with speed and endurance. That interaction leads to various types of strength. Whereas sprinters are trained in maximum strength and resilience, long-distance runners require a generally lower level of strength—but they need it for a longer period of time. This is an issue of strength endurance. Strength training for endurance athletes must therefore address this specific type of demand. An extreme increase in maximum strength, such as that produced by bodybuilding or weight lifting, would entail no advantages for distance runners. On the contrary, it would involve significant disadvantages such as greater body weight and faster tiring of the muscles.

An increase in strength can be accomplished principally through muscle hypertrophy, or thickening of the muscle. High and especially long and repeated muscle tension leads to hypertrophy. However, more strength can also be produced without an increase in size by optimizing coordination within and between muscles. Intermuscular refers to cooperation among different muscles or, in other words, an improvement in the technique of performing a movement. Intramuscular involves the number of motor units (nerve and muscle fibers) as a percentage within a muscle that can be stimulated at the same time. In the absence of training, the rate is somewhere around 20 percent. However, top-level athletes in strength sports can synchronize almost all their fibers and approach 100 percent. Specific

types of strength training develop these qualities without leading to pronounced increases in muscle size. Examples are resilience training involving short-term muscle tensing, performing the movements as quickly as possible, and lengthy rest breaks.

Measuring Strength

Isokinetic strength-measuring devices have proven their worth in gauging and graphically displaying muscle strength. Adapters are used to measure various levels of movement in the major joints. The subject of the test moves the appropriate joint (in what is known as concentric contraction) in a procedure where the device provides variable resistance but never

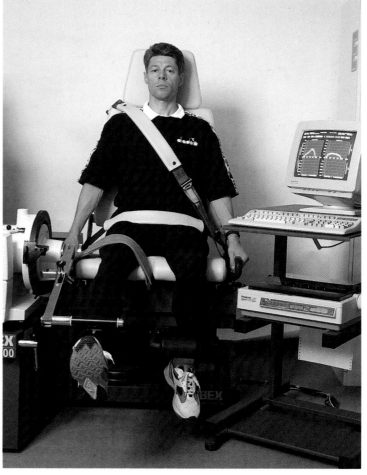

Isokinetic strength measurement.

greater than the applied strength. This is measured and graphed. The speed of the movements can be chosen at will.

Alternatively, the lever is moved by the machine. The subject attempts to apply enough resistance to stop the motion (eccentric contraction).

Amounts and Methods of Strength Training

The appropriate amount of strength training is best determined according to the athlete's recognized goals. The greater the weights used, the higher the amount of maximum strength. The greater the number of repetitions (with lighter weights), the greater the effect with respect to strength endurance.

An especially appropriate type of structure involves *circuit training*. Different muscle groups are called into play at various stations. Depending on the type of exercise, different types of strength can be emphasized.

As with running, strength training can be divided into extensive and intensive interval methods. The extensive type is distinguished by a high number of repetitions of a particular exercise (up to 30), short rest breaks, and fairly light weights. The athlete's own body and light weights such as sandbags and a bar provide enough resistance. All important muscle groups in the body can be addressed in this way. Based on the broad range of exercises, a good foundation is established where strength endurance is of central importance. The adaptation—an increase in strength—is achieved more slowly, but it is more stable. It also does not deteriorate so quickly if strength training is interrupted for a while. These types of training are especially good for children, youngsters, and fitness athletes; they can also occasionally be used for endurance by competitive athletes.

The *intensive interval method* involves using fewer repetitions per station (up to 12) with heavier weights. This requires a somewhat more costly type of training because you need a weight room or fitness center. Since this type of strength training is especially good for improving resilience, it involves explosive movements. Rest breaks between sets should be fairly long, and the number of repetitions should be low. These two types of training methods can be incorporated into circuit training.

A very demanding type of training is the *control method*. A circuit of perhaps eight stations is set up. Each exercise is done for 30 seconds, followed by a 45-second rest break for changing to the next piece of apparatus. At every station, an attempt is made to do the greatest possible number of repetitions. After a complete circuit, the numbers of repetitions are added up to produce a simple means of checking

Goal	Repetitions	Sets	Break between sets
Maximum strength	2–4	1–2	Very long
Pronounced hypertrophy (bodybuilding)	8–12	2–3	Long
Mild hypertrophy (body shaping)	14–18	2–3	Medium
Strength endurance	25–40	2–4	Short

performance. Periods of work and rest should be kept to about 1:1.5 or 1:2 minutes. If this type of training is done properly, it contributes to maximum strength, resilience, and strength endurance all at the same time. In addition to local fatigue there is a general fatigue for the training also affects the circulatory system. This method also imposes very high physical and psychological demands, so it should be built up to gradually through a training regimen of several years' duration using methods that are less taxing.

Strength training involves longer recovery periods than endurance training does. So it does not make sense to do strength training every day, especially for runners. An individual strength-training program can be built into training two to three times a week and preferably in blocks (e.g., two to three times a week for four to six weeks a year). Only for excessive deficiencies in the movement apparatus that are attributable to a lack of muscle strength should strength training be given more emphasis in the course of a year's workouts. In that case, running should be cut back accordingly.

Periodizing Strength Training

In strength training, it is a good idea to vary the type and intensity of the workload regularly. This keeps you from doing the same exercises twice a week year in and year out. You can apply the same type of periodizing to strength training as to running (see page 49). The following structure makes sense with one or two workouts per week. By starting in November with the beginning of Preparation Period I and up to the end of December, basic conditioning is done according to the

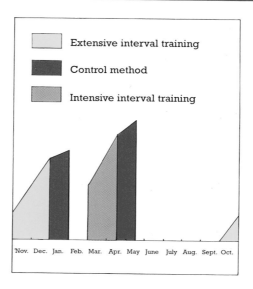

Sample periodizing of strength training for runners in the course of a training year.

extensive interval method. In the following month and a half, the control method (with other exercises as explained earlier) is used. After a break of about four weeks, the intensive interval method is used in Preparation Period II from mid-March through the beginning of May. After that, the control method is used again for about four weeks. Within the individual phases, an attempt should continually be made to increase the number of repetitions (extensive interval method), the weight (intensive interval method), or the number of repetitions per time unit (control method).

There are no limits to the imaginativeness of an athlete in setting up a personal training program. The following sections will present some examples that can be used in exercising important muscle groups. A number of training aids will be required, which are usually available in athletic clubs.

Devices for exercises using your own body weight:
Jump rope, climbing pole, climbing rope, wall bars, stairs, high bar, rings, parallel bars, gymnastics facilities, and others.

Exercises involving light resistance: Exercises with a partner, medicine ball, sandbags, dumbbells, barbells, and assorted types of strength machines.

Strength Training for Adolescents

The value of strength training for an adolescent's musculoskeletal system is unchallenged. Adolescence is perfectly suited for improving speed and agility and for learning fairly difficult movements. General, well-developed muscle strength is the best foundation for these capabilities and for subsequent endurance training. Strength is also a good protection for the adolescent musculoskeletal system against strains and improper stresses. The system does not require tremendous amounts of maximum strength training, which would only endanger tendons, joint cartilage, and the spinal column. It is much better to develop all of the body's large muscle groups extensively, such as through extensive interval circuit training. The control method is also useful for increasing resilience, but this should be introduced only gradually. (For information about the individual methods, see page 88.) Both methods are appropriate for general strengthening of the musculoskeletal system and increasing its resistance. Children and adolescents should, however, undertake regular strength training only after consulting with a doctor.

In particular, statics, function, and X rays of the spine should reveal no serious abnormalities. The spine and growth areas are at particular risk in the growth phases. This sensitivity is heightened in the case of developmental delays and Scheuermann's disease (osteochondrosis).

Deformities, static pressure problems (e.g., unequal leg length), structural problems such as Osgood-Schlatter disease, and similar illnesses and irregularities of the musculoskeletal system must be identified early so that they can be counteracted effectively.

Strength Training on Weight Machines

Training on weight machines offers an important advantage over any other kind of strength training: exact loads and reproducibility. Complete training programs can be designed and recorded with respect to scope (total amount of weight lifted), number of sets, and number of repetitions with individual weights. Even the intensity of the stimulus on each piece of apparatus can be documented precisely—that is, the number of repetitions per unit of time.

A further advantage, especially for beginners, is the fact that many exercise machines help reduce improper movements—as long as they are adjusted properly, that is, according to the user's body size, leverage, and movement axes. Free weights require considerably more coordination. However, even in using weight machines, basic principles of posture must be observed (head erect, shoulders back, back straight, tension in upper-body muscles, and so forth).

A workout could be structured according to the intensive interval method as follows:

Three sets of eight to 12 repetitions per station. Long breaks between sets (e.g., five minutes). Goal: hypertrophy training.

If you wish to train using the extensive interval method, the weights are lighter and the repetitions are higher. For example, three sets of 25 to 40 repetitions per station. Short rest break between sets (e.g., one to two minutes). Goal: strength endurance training.

① Leg Press (Functional Press)

Preferably while lying on your back or in a semireclined position, a weight (foot plate) is moved by straightening the legs. This involves the hip muscles (m. gluteus maximus), the quadriceps, and the lower-leg muscles (gastrocnemius and soleus). During the entire exercise, the joints should be held in line with one another (especially keep the knees stable!). Tensing the stomach muscles takes pressure off the lumbar vertebrae. Knee bend should not exceed a right angle.

This exercise and some others should be done one leg at a time in order to provide a precise, separate test of each leg's strength and reveal if there is any difference between the two.

② Knee Bends

In a sitting position, bend the knee against the resistance and pull the lever downward. Be sure to keep your back straight. This strengthens the hamstring muscle (ischiocrural or knee-bending musculature).

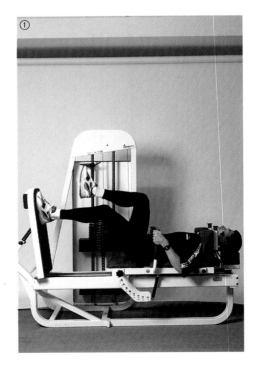

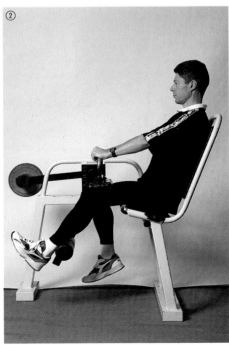

④ Hip Conditioning

As you stand on one leg, press outward with the active leg. Keep the anchor leg, the pelvis, and the upper body still, and avoid making any compensating movements. This serves to strengthen the bottom muscles (gluteus medius and minimus).

⑤ When you press the active leg inward (the opposite movement), the muscles of the inside thigh (adductors/m. gracilis) are strengthened.

⑥ Cable Pull for Trapezius

Weight machines with cables offer the greatest variety in training. All major muscle groups can be developed by changing the weight, body position, and settings. Movements can be done freely in space and in any direction.

Developing the trapezius muscle is good for posture and stability in the shoulders. Arms are rotated outward in order to activate the muscles around the shoulder blades; then they are drawn rearward and

③ Leg Raises

With feet on the floor and upper body lying on the bench, straighten the hip of the active leg against the resistance. This strengthens mainly the gluteus maximus muscles. Keep your upper body from moving by tensing your stomach muscles.

Important note: When the support leg is slightly bent, the upper body must be at the same level as the axis of the hip joint.

downward. The upper body should be kept erect and still while doing this exercise. Tip the pelvis forward, tense your muscles to keep the lumbar vertebrae still (back slightly dished), keep the shoulders back and head up.

⑦ Shoulder Stabilizers
Strengthening the muscles around the shoulder blades is effective in combating a rounded back, problems with neck vertebrae, and headaches that result from poor posture and monotonous jobs (sitting down!). From a forward starting position, the upper arms are drawn rearward and horizontally against resistance. This strengthens the shoulder blade stabilizers (the rhomboids or shoulder blade lifters) and slightly stretches the chest muscles.

⑧ Knee Bends with Free Weights
The bar rests across the shoulders. Use a bent squat bar, or pad the bar with a towel.
   Place the feet about shoulder width apart and slightly pointed

outward. Keep the knees oriented straight ahead (i.e., without any movement outward or inward!) and your bottom pointed to the rear. Keep your back slightly dished and

the lumbar vertebrae stable by flexing the muscles in that area. Keep your head up.

You must keep your back straight as you do the knee bends. Any bending of the spine toward the front involves risk of injury. In order to prevent excessive stress on the knees, especially the kneecaps, the squats should be done only to a right angle in the knees.

Low-Dose Strength Training

Strength training can be done in adequate amounts to address the purposes of endurance and fitness runners even if there are no costly weight machines available.

A small but very good training tool that will fit into any sports or travel bag is the Thera-band. This involves a series of latex bands in various color-coded strengths. Even when they are stretched forcefully, the resistance of the bands increases gradually, and this is a major advantage with exercises that involve a lot of movement.

These exercises can be done according to the number of repetitions (e.g., three sets of 15 to 40 reps per station) or the duration of the workload (e.g., three sets using 20 to 40 seconds of load and 40 to 60 seconds of rest break per station).

① Basic Position

This is the starting position for many types of exercises and an ideal standing position stabilized by muscles. The feet are placed a little wider apart than the hips and slightly pointed outward. Knees are slightly bent, and hips, kneecaps, and feet are all aligned with one another. The pelvis is tipped forward, and the slight dishing that naturally occurs in the lower back is secured by flexing the stomach muscles and spinal erectors; it also extends upward to the middle of the vertebrae in the chest area. The shoulders are held back, and the muscles around the shoulder blades are tensed. The upper arms are held horizontal and the forearms vertical.

The head is erect, and the gaze is directed straight forward.

② **Posture Stabilizers**

By starting with the basic position, the upper arms are brought rearward against the resistance of the Thera-band until it seems like the inner edges of the shoulder blades are touching. This exercise strengthens the triceps muscles (m. triceps brachii) and the so-called posture stabilizers (the muscles between the shoulder blades, especially the lifters, [m. levator scapulae], and the rhomboidal muscles [m. rhomboidei]). This exercise is effective in counteracting the rounding of the shoulders that is caused by continuous sitting.

③ **Strengthening Shoulders and Stabilizing Posture**

In a sitting position with the legs slightly spread and pointed outward, pelvis tipped forward, pronounced dishing in the lumbar vertebrae, shoulders held back, and head erect, the arms are pushed outward against the resistance of the band (in what is known as an abduction movement). This improves posture and strengthens the deltoid and supraspinatus muscles on the shoulder blades to a significant degree. To a lesser extent, it also affects the biceps (m. biceps brachii).

④ **Strengthening Stomach Muscles**

As you lie on your back, raise the thighs vertically and hold the lower legs horizontally (with right angles in hips and knees). By tensing the stomach muscles, the lumbar vertebrae are pressed against the floor. Then the torso is raised up but only to the point where the shoulder blades are lifted from the floor. The head is kept aligned with the torso, and the gaze is directed upward. Arms are rotated outward so that the palms face up.

⑤ Pelvis Stability 1 (Abductors)

With every step, the pelvis is lifted up by the flexing of the muscles in the bottom on the side of the support leg (using the medium and small gluteals, gluteus medius and minimus). This provides enough room to swing ahead freely beneath the body. To strengthen the so-called hip extenders (or hip abductors), first assume the basic stance shown above. The active leg is moved outward and rearward against the resistance of the Thera-band. The knee of the support leg is bent; the active leg is straight at the knee, and the toes are pointed in. The movement is a little like pushing off in cross-country skiing, speed skating, or roller blading. This exercise strengthens the gluteal muscles and is especially good for strengthening the support leg (calf muscles and knee stabilization).

⑥ Pelvis Stability 2 (Adductors)

The adductors (the thin group of muscles on the inside of the thigh) are used to bring the legs together.

They also help stabilize the pelvis by bringing the body's center of gravity over the support leg. With poor abductors and good adductors, runners *overstep*, or cross over an imaginary centerline with the support leg. You can strengthen these muscles by using practically the same setup as with the previous exercise. However, this time the leg is brought toward the body against the resistance from the Thera-band so that it crosses in front of the support leg.

⑦ Knee Stability and Hip Stretches

By far the most important muscle group for stabilizing the knee and relieving stress on the kneecap is what is referred to as the ischiocrural musculature (from the sitting bone ischia to the calf/crus) on the back of the thigh. These muscles can be effectively strengthened without the use of weight machines by bridging, preferably one leg at a time. The heel of one foot is pressed forcefully against the floor, and the other leg is lifted up. Arms are held across the

chest. By tensing the ischiocrural muscles, the bottom is lifted up from the floor. Caution: this muscle group is often fairly weak and may tend to cramp. A safety valve in this instance is the corresponding stretching exercise (see page 160, number 3).

Concurrently, the large gluteal muscle (gluteus maximus) is strengthened; it straightens the hip joint and keeps the body's center of gravity high while running. (People who "sit" while they run usually have weak gluteus maximus muscles.)

Dangers from Strength Training

Strength training is not without danger. The heavier the weights, especially with barbell training, the greater the threat of injury to muscles, bones, tendons, and ligaments. The main reason for injuries is improper technique; another cause is tackling too much weight without adequate preparation. As long as a couple of basic rules of posture are observed, serious injuries can largely be avoided—assuming, of course, a healthy musculoskeletal system.

1. In strength training, weights should be increased only gradually.
2. Especially with adolescents, but also with adults, a varied, basic, general conditioning program should precede weight training. In other words, first general, then specific strength training.
3. Learning the right technique for every exercise is the basic requirement for avoiding injury; this is also the right way to get the benefit from the training.
4. Strength training should never be done without a good warm-up. Between individual exercises or sets, the muscles should be kept loose and warm.
5. Be sure to choose your workload in conjunction with your age, physical condition, and technical ability. Adolescents should first begin weight training, for example, no earlier than age 14 or 15 in order to avoid injuries to a musculoskeletal system that is not yet mature. (Examples include torn tendons, aseptic bone necrosis, structural loosening, and injuries to vertebrae). Regular orthopedic checkups are always advisable.

■ Developing Coordination

Even though running is the most natural thing in the world, it consists of a very complex series of movements. So it is not a primitive affair, as some detractors claim. Nearly all the muscles in the body are integrated into the movement. It takes a very good sense of kinetics to channel all of one's strength effectively into forward motion. Superfluous movements use up energy needlessly and lead to cramps and premature fatigue.

Of course, not everyone can run like Sebastian Coe or Steve Cram, the great British middle-distance runners, since anthropometric qualities and body size vary so much. However, even if there is no such thing as an ideal running style, the world's best runners still display some common

Marc Nenow, Markus Ryffel, and Christoph Herle know the importance of regular coordination exercises.

ground that can be used for reference and that can be an example and an incentive for runners to improve their style.

Sample Exercises for Coordination Training

For that purpose, here are examples of some coordination exercises that have a secure place in the training program of many successful runners. When done regularly, they help improve one's sense of movement, especially for running, and they enhance awareness of individual movement phases. These include such things as pushing off with the feet, lifting the knees, flight phase, and planting the feet. The exercises should be done regularly and fairly frequently, ideally two to three times per week. You should start with an easy warm-up but not a tiring workout. Otherwise, the receptiveness and reactive abilities of important neuromotor centers may be adversely affected.

① Short Skips (Ankle Work)

Head and torso are held upright, eyes looking straight ahead, shoulders relaxed and not raised, arms swinging parallel. At fairly high cadence, movements are short. When the arms swing forward and back, elbows should always be held at a right angle. Hands are held in a loose fist but not clenched.

Hips and lumbar vertebrae are straight. Set the feet down parallel; the forward foot first lands on the ball, but the heel also touches the ground in the push-off phase. Each stride is very short, approximately half a foot length. The important thing is to use the whole range of movement in the upper ankle by bending and straightening the foot. The pushing-off motion strengthens the calf muscles.

First work on proper form. Then continually increase cadence.

② Knee Lifts

With knee lifts, a runner is almost doing forced skipping where lifting the knees up to horizontal is more important than cadence. Head and torso are upright and very slightly inclined forward. The eyes look straight ahead. Shoulders, arms, and hands are brought into play as the runner skips. Hips are straight. After a gentle start, the push-off with the support leg is intensified to the horizontal level.

It is important to keep the hips and the bottom in the right position; the pelvis must be pushed forward to keep the center of gravity where it belongs. Do not sit back! Here, too, you should advance moderately, only about one foot length per step. You can also finish up this exercise by leaning forward more with the torso (hips extended farther!), gradually increasing the strides, and changing over to a controlled sprint.

③ Hop Running

This exercise is well known to children at play; they have no trouble at all imitating this movement. At first, grown-ups sometimes have trouble changing the stride (left-left, right-right).

Torso and head are held upright. Eyes look straight ahead. Shoulders are relaxed. Arms swing parallel. Move the upper arms forcefully up to horizontal in the forward and rearward swing. Maintain a right angle in the elbow.

Lumbar vertebrae and hips are upright and straight. Feet are planted parallel, heel first, then roll the length of the foot and push off with the ball of the foot (the forefoot). Swing the leg forward forcefully, and lift the thigh to horizontal. The lower leg is relaxed, with a right angle in the ankle. No landing on the heel! The rhythm of the step involves a hop and a step. That is, an exaggerated hop on the same leg (a left-left hop) is followed by a relaxed jump and a switch to the other foot (step, left-right).

It is important to push off cleanly and forcefully for a coordinated hop that comes from the entire leg and torso, similar to the strong arm movements used for support in the long jump.

At first, work on form. Then exaggerate the movement with

the longest possible flight phase or hop.

④ **Side Springs**
Side springs strengthen important muscles and improve pelvis stability in running. They involve the abductors in extending the leg to the side and the adductors in bringing the legs together.

⑤ **Bounding (Stride Jumps)**
Begin this movement slowly and with lots of spring. Head is erect, eyes look straight ahead. The torso leans gently forward. Lumbar vertebrae and hips are straight. Feet land parallel. After the support phase, push off forcefully with the forefoot. Bring the advancing leg forward forcefully up to horizontal. Lower leg and foot are relaxed during the flight phase (no landing on the heel!). In the push-off phase, the support leg is totally extended. Shoulders are relaxed; arms are moved forcefully and parallel to one another for momentum and balance.

100

Recovery Measures

As already explained elsewhere (see page 35), rest periods are an important part of training. They allow the entire body to recover and build new reserves. Even popular speech recognizes that you can draw from the well only so often before it goes dry. The goal of some simple regenerative measures is to keep the well from going dry and to shorten the necessary recovery time.

Adequate recovery begins with as much uniformity as possible in the daily routine of activity and rest. The more regular that meals, work, training, and sleep are followed in the day's rhythm, the better the body can adjust to them. (For more on the importance of balanced nutrition, see page 114ff.) People vary greatly in their need for sleep, which generally decreases with age. Eight hours a night is a good average for working people between the ages of 25 and 55, but individuals can vary greatly from that amount. The bedroom should be well ventilated, darkened, and quiet; the mattress should be firm and the pillow flat.

It is not really true that sleep before midnight is the best. That is only a misinterpretation of the fact that going to bed at the same time guarantees a deeper sleep.

The frequently changing demands to which people in today's working world are increasingly subjected lead to rapid exhaustion of energy reserves and to the onset of physical and psychological problems. People have to let their bodies recover and reestablish their mental vigor. This goal is achieved most quickly and fundamentally through a so-called phycho-autonomic decoupling, that is, through freeing yourself from all

It is important to push off actively from the ground. This also helps with coordination, sense of balance, and learning to keep the center of gravity in the right place. After a restrained start, effort should be increased to create a long, high flight phase. You can finish up by increasing the cadence and switching over into an energetic, well-coordinated run.

⑥ Step-Ups (Runs of Increasing Intensity)

All coordination exercises, just like other exercises, should simply help to make running as efficient as possible. A program like the one described above should end with a few runs.

Start off gradually, slowly enough so that you can control integrated functions (position of head and arms, push-off with the feet, and so forth). Then you can force the speed to end in a less-than-all-out sprint in the last 65 feet (20 m) of a 295- to 395-foot (90 to 120 m) stretch. Always try to stay loose and run with good coordination, even in a sprint!

burdensome problems that may be weighing you down. Sleep becomes deeper, you fall asleep more quickly, and you wake up refreshed. In phases of extreme physical and nervous stress, this regeneration process can become disturbed when your thoughts will not give you any rest. Many people, including numerous athletes, have been able to help themselves with methods involving concentrated relaxation exercises such as autogenous training, progressive muscle relaxation based on the work of Jacobson, yoga, and other meditation techniques. When using these techniques, you cannot expect success within a couple of days. However, over the long-term, they are more effective than medicines in treating nervous overstimulation and sleep disturbances, and they involve no harmful side effects.

Cooldown Runs

A warm-up program (see page 109) is useful in preparing the musculoskeletal system for the demands of training and competition. Similarly, a cooldown run serves as an active recovery measure after a workout and as the most effective way to increase blood circulation and the attendant regeneration. Stretching exercises (see pages 77–78) should also be integrated into the cooldown process in order to keep fatigued muscles from shortening and to return the muscles to their normal tone. In particular, this can be used from the outset to keep the calf muscles and hamstrings from becoming too tight. The importance of a regenerative run was already pointed out on page 41. It is the ideal antidote to the undeniable intensity of a training workout.

Massage

The various forms of massage (connective tissue, relaxation, kneading or stroking massages) relax the body and promote circulation. They can be used to treat tight muscles or prevent their occurrence. Before the massage, the muscles should be warmed up by means of a hot bath, warm air, or poultices or, even better, 15 or 20 minutes of easy jogging.

However, I do not believe that it is adequate for prevention of injuries to get a massage once or twice a week without taking into consideration whether you are relaxed or fresh from a hard workout or a competition. Frankly, massages are recovery measures that should be used for a specific purpose. An overstrained, fatigued muscle does not always respond positively when it is kneaded right at the conclusion of a demanding workload.

Underwater massages have proven very effective in treating tight muscles. The effect that the warm water produces is a complete relaxation in the muscle. This, in turn, permits a particularly deep massage. The intensity of the massage can be varied according to the strength of the jet of water.

Baths

Hot bathwater can produce intensive, deep circulatory stimulation (at temperatures of 99 to 104 degrees Fahrenheit/37 to 40 degrees Centigrade for 15 to 20 minutes). It is a good idea to put in some bathwater additives such as hay blossoms, spruce needles, or balm. This also promotes mental and psychological relaxation. Equally effective is a swim in a thermal or saltwater pool (water temperature between 86 and 92 degrees Fahrenheit/30 and 33 degrees Centigrade). The motor ability of the blood vessels (expansion and contraction) can be regulated even more effectively with alternating hot and cold showers or baths. For instance, one can use a lower leg bath with three changes from hot (about five minutes each) to cold (one to two minutes each). Always end with a cold bath! A sauna works similarly, but the effect on the entire body is much more pronounced (stimulation of the circulatory system and metabolism). Used regularly (at least once a week), a sauna also promotes recovery and purificaiton; just the same, it is not a substitute for training and is not effective in weight reduction, since it only involves fluid loss.

Fitness and Sports

Other sports practiced to complement running, or instead of running, can be of value to runners in many ways.

Various forms of strength training, gymnastics, and swimming are great for developing overall physical fitness. They also help reduce strains and improper stresses that may occur from uninterrupted running workouts. (Strength training is treated in detail starting on page 86.)

These types of sports are a good complement to running. They improve flexibility, coordination, and strength, thereby reducing the danger of injury from running. In addition, they involve otherwise neglected muscle groups.

Also, injuries that make running unadvisable or altogether impossible may call for another type of endurance training. The best ones are cycling, cross-country skiing, and swimming/aqua jogging. They produce great results on the circulatory system but take it easy on the musculoskeletal system. With these types of sports, the danger of injury is exceptionally low. In order to prevent muscular atrophy (or decrease), complementary strength training is very valuable. Many athletes have gotten through layoffs due to injury so successfully by using such a program that very soon after they were cured, they were able to resume their running at full capacity.

As a result, the negative effects of a forced layoff can be kept to a minimum.

This can also serve as a psychological and physical change from the sometimes monotonous running workouts. Game sports such as basketball, soccer, tennis, Ping-Pong, and badminton offer group experiences and motivation for competition.

The training effect on the circulatory system with most games is quite minor, despite the exertion that people experience subjectively. We should also point out that most game sports, especially soccer, handball, and even basketball, volleyball, tennis, and squash, involve a relatively high risk of injury—especially for runners who rarely practice these sports and therefore may not have complete mastery over the technical skills they require. So if you feel like taking a crack at some sport on a Saturday-night team, think about what you are doing—and ask your teammates and opponents to take it easy on you.

Competition

For performance athletes, competition is the most important goal of all training and effort. However, even many fitness athletes regularly take part in competition even though they realize that they are never in top form when they step up to the starting line. For them it is not a question of their absolute best performance or fantastic times for the record book. It is the personal, relative performance that is more important, compared to their earlier results or those of their training partners, and always in relation to their personal training effort.

Oftentimes, competition is simply a change of pace from regular training and a special experience with like-minded people. Competition involves many facets that make it stimulating. Striving to perform, the desire to improve and to surpass others—these are part of human nature. Running also offers the opportunity to live out these needs and to release tensions that, of course, must be subdued or sublimated in the course of living together in our civilized society. Friendly competition with other runners or against the clock is always a struggle with one's self. It takes us to limits that normally are closed to us and opens up to us a personal, age-old, yet new part of life. Competition blends physical and mental experiences of the highest intensity. Joy and dejection, satisfaction and disappointment, take on previously unknown dimensions. The level of performance plays a supreme role. The elation that a casual runner feels after a three-and-a-half-hour marathon can be as complete as that experienced by a competitive runner who runs the same course an hour faster. So

In major international competitions, the distance events have been dominated by African runners—especially from Ethopia.

performance cannot be viewed as an absolute, but always in relation to the conditions that give rise to it.

Planning for Competition

You should never go to the starting line unprepared if you want a competition to be the most successful experience possible.

The first step is to determine the goals and high points for the upcoming competition year. You can determine important points with the help of an outline plan. Keep it flexible enough so you have room for any development meets that may come up on short notice.

Good planning for competition also avoids programming in boredom and burnout from too many competitions, or from always running the same events. Variety is as important in competition as it is in training. Runners who know how to keep a fresh outlook will feel fresh physically and stay ready for competition.

Whereas topflight marathon runners will compete in two or, at the most, three races per year at that special distance, middle- and long-distance runners periodize their training with one or two peaks. One peak involves reaching the best competitive form just once a year for a limited period of time. Two peaks, on the other hand, involves reaching two high points, which may be weighted differently—for example, a cross-country season in winter and a road-running season in the summer. The type of plan that any runner chooses depends on individual factors. Anyone who prefers to race frequently rather than going for months without competing should choose a two-peak plan. Other runners need to take the fall and winter off so they can recover for the next year.

Physical Preparation for Racing

An important competition should be an exceptional situation for the athlete, toward which all training is directed. That means that it is not just another type of training, but it rather requires an exceptional type of physical and mental preparation.

The amount of training is reduced at the right time so that the runner can go to the start thoroughly rested and in full possession of all strength. Before a race, it is better to train less if there is any doubt. There is no sense in trying to soothe your conscience through additional last-minute workouts. A couple of fairly short workouts with a little more emphasis on speed are often good preparation for the higher cadence in a race.

Otherwise, the usual even pace of life should be maintained in order to avoid placing any further demands on the body. This applies especially to sleep and nutrition.

Mental Preparation for Racing

In parallel with physical preparation, runners should also prepare mentally. Observant spectators can see almost daily the ways in which the mental qualities of a competitor affect performance.

The traits that help runners focus on competition seem almost contradictory. They are motivated but not fixated, at once expectantly tense yet composed in their tension, and focused on the essential yet alert and receptive.

Underlying that is a competition-affirming, performance-motivated fundamental outlook that is characterized by a healthy self-awareness. The imminent race should cause no anxiety but should provide resolution and proof of the runner's ability to perform; it should also be fun.

Focusing on the impending race should start early, for the last 24 hours are the most important ones. Experienced competitors always describe in the same way how in that period of time they turn their thoughts more and more toward the race, considering it from all sides and concentrating on it. This mental adjustment also involves a physical one. The autonomic functions gradually become programmed for performance. Appetite decreases, the digestive process speeds up, and the circulatory system is increasingly stimulated. A general tension begins to develop, which may be dismissed as annoying nervousness but which is necessary preparation for the event.

Runners can prepare themselves very well for the impending race by continually visualizing the important stages of the competitive situation such as the start, a tough climb, and the sprint for the finish—all handled successfully. That is what we refer to as positive thinking. The people who use it to their advantage could teach the rest of us a thing or two. Nervousness and apprehension are reduced when thoughts of failure and poor performance are banished. One's psyche can be conditioned through mental exercises. In other words, it is possible over time to put yourself into a position to see certain things in a positive light. Many athletes use this form of preparation for competition or use the method to

One-Peak Periodizing	Two-Peak Periodizing
Transition Period	
Preparation Period I (general)	Preparation Period I (general)
	Preparation Period II (special)
Preparation Period II (special)	Competition Period I
Competition Period I (developing form)	Competition Period II (general and special)
Competition Period II (maintaining form)	Competition Period II

Periodizing with one and two peaks (variations based on Letzelter).

The best position for relaxing psyche and circulatory system after a race.

You should stick to accustomed, easily digested foods—in other words, no cold orange juice or strong coffee if you are accustomed to drinking only tea.

If the race is scheduled for the afternoon or the late evening, as with many international track and field festivals, the accustomed times for going to bed, getting up, and eating meals can be adhered to. Nearly all long-distance runners loosen up a little after breakfast on race day, with a regenerative run of 15 to 20 minutes, some stretching exercises, and a few incremental

get through critical phases during the race. One of Germany's best marathoners reported that before each competition, he came up with an answer for every question that might arise during the race—such as "Why are you doing this?" and "Why don't you just stand still?"

◼ The Day of the Race

Many road races, particularly in the United States, start very early in the morning, between 7:00 and 10:00. That means that the race day starts on the day before. Given that, in the afternoon or early evening you should have a carbohydrate-rich meal and go to bed relatively early but not right after eating. On the morning of the race, the runners usually get up at least three to four hours before starting time to give their body enough time to get into the swing of things. This process can be helped along by taking a short walk or jog, and by doing a few stretching and relaxation exercises. It is also a good idea to have a light breakfast—as a last batch of carbohydrates—and to get rid of that uncomfortable feeling of emptiness in the stomach.

runs. Most athletes also rest up a little after the last meal, four to six hours before the race. You should be careful not to sleep too much (perhaps 30 to 60 minutes) and be back on your feet at least two-and-a-half hours before the run. Otherwise, the race may be all over before you are back up to speed.

The actual warm-up program starts from 40 minutes to an hour before the start. In famous marathons that draw thousands of competitors (such as New York, Berlin, and London), you have to show up at the start very early to

get a good spot. Of course, that forces you into starting your warm-up runs earlier. In addition, it is often very difficult to maintain the effect of the warm-up if you have to wait around on a couple of square feet of pavement for a half hour or more. The only solution is to do a couple of exercises in place (light skipping, hopping, or stretching), be patient, and put on a smile. Save your aggression for the race. In warming up, nearly all top-level runners follow this pattern. They begin with easy jogging for ten to 20 minutes. Then they do stretching exercises for five to 15 minutes, perhaps interspersing them with more jogging. It is good to end with some incremental runs at race speed or slightly over. That should leave about 15 minutes to change clothes, maybe take another bathroom break, and then report to the start. It is important not to rush the warm-up and to maintain the concentration on the competition up to the end. That is why it is better for many runners to warm up by themselves.

The stretching exercises are a good opportunity to gather your thoughts. During the incremental runs, the built-up tension can be transformed into a fairly high cadence. After warming up, you should be stimulated and ready to perform but not dripping with sweat and out of breath at the start.

It is not advisable to use circulation-enhancing substances to aid or even replace the warm-up process, as some people do. They increase circulation only to the surface blood vessels and have no effect on the deeper vessels in the muscles. We have had better results in very cold weather with a thin film of baby oil, which can help hold the heat in, especially in wet or cold weather.

In contrast to most Western runners, African athletes prefer to warm up as a group.

Strategy and Tactics

A basic requirement for effective race strategy is a knowledge of your own capabilities, so you will need to do an objective self-evaluation. This will serve as a point of reference in planning your time before the race. Is it your intention to beat specific opponents, or is it more important to turn in a good time? Should you pace yourself from start to finish or muster all your strength for the final sprint? Is this a new distance for you? Are you familiar with the course? Where do you expect to find the critical points where you might save some energy by running more conservatively or where you might run aggressively and shake off your opponents? Are there any problems with temperature, humidity, or wind conditions? Some people like to plan out every step as much as possible. Others prefer a rough game plan that leaves room for spontaneous decisions dictated by the running conditions. A runner's character shows in competition. One runs tentatively and conservatively, and another charges ahead energetically. All runners need to play their own strengths to best advantage and proceed in such a way that their weaknesses remain in the background.

The 3,000-meter hurdle event at the European Championships in Stuttgart in August of 1986 provided a marvelous, dramatic example of race strategy. The Italian runner Francesco Panetta, one of the strongest runners in the field but not among the most talented kickers in the final stretch, took off like a jackrabbit in order to discourage his opponents and wear them down with the high speed. He also knew that he would have more problems than his opponents with technique over the hurdles if he continued to run in the pack. Since none of the favorites wanted to go with Panetta's starting speed, his initial lead in places exceeded 165 feet (50 m). With a lap and a half to go, it looked like no one would catch him. However, then Patriz Ilg saw that he just might have a chance to catch Panetta if he pursued him. He decided to take the initiative and bring the main field with him, even though that required abandoning his original plan of a short sprint to the finish from second or third position. Patriz Ilg in fact succeeded in catching and passing Panetta, but Hagen Melzer from (then) East Germany was actually in the better position to pull off a successful attack in the last 330 feet (100 m).

Patriz Ilg, who had already been counting on victory, understandably let up a little and was in turn passed again by the amazing Panetta.

This run can serve as an example of how tactical behavior can influence the end result of a race. You can keep replaying endless possibilities involving "ifs" and "should haves," but you cannot escape reality. Competition, with its varied and imponderable nature and chesslike moves, often presents unforeseen changes that must be seized in fractions of a second. Anyone who is not influenced by nervousness and other hindrances and can make the right moves through clear thinking or good instincts can overcome, to a certain degree, inferiority in running.

(Top) Page 110: The fastest middle-distance runner of all times: Nourredine Morceli from Algeria (here pictured next to the 1,500-meter Olympic champion from Barcelona, the Spaniard Fermin Cacho).

(Below) Finish of the 3,000-meter hurdle finals at the 1986 Stuttgard European Championship; from left: Francesco Panetta (Italy), Patriz Ilg (Germany), and Hagen Melzer (then East Germany).

Inner relaxation and concentration are part of preparation right before a race.

■ After the Race

The results of a race naturally influence how a runner feels physically and mentally after crossing the finish line. We have all seen photos where overjoyed victors take a victory lap at a scarcely reduced speed while a defeated opponent lies on the track struggling for breath. Our psyche makes it possible for us to endure tremendous physical strain when we experience euphoria; and conversely, a defeat can make for very painful experiences. Just the same, after

every run there are some unmistakable, measurable parameters that indicate the strain of the preceding run. Carbohydrate reserves are used up, waste products in the body (such as lactic acid and urine) are elevated, and even the hormone reservoirs that control activity (including the suprarenal glands and the testicles) are partly depleted. To restore as quickly as possible the capacity to perform, the regeneration measures should begin as quickly as possible after the end of the race.

In order to bring circulation back to resting levels and foster improved peripheral circulation, especially to the leg muscles, it is a good idea to jog or walk for 15 minutes to a half hour right after the race—slowly enough so that you can easily maintain a conversation. Stretching and loosening-up exercises also help counteract muscle tightness.

Runners who are so tired after a race that they can scarcely stay on their legs, or who collapse altogether, are best off to rest up a little in the ideal relaxation position (lying on the back, perhaps with knees drawn up).

Once your heart rate is closer to resting, lie flat on your back with your arms stretched out beside your body and your lower legs horizontal against a raised surface to facilitate venous circulation back to the heart. Try to relax completely physically and mentally, breathe deeply, and get rid of all your ballast: pressure to perform, competitive stress, and any other kind of pressure. Another active regeneration measure that helps with circulation and removal of metabolic substances is a hot bath. Invigorating bathwater additives or even a handful of salt can heighten the effect. A relaxing massage or a visit to the sauna have a similar effect, but the latter should not be done immediately after a race.

Aside from the steps that address waste disposal, the depleted energy reservoirs also need to be replenished. In the following section, we will treat the topic of eating after a race.

Drinking lots of very cold drinks is something you should not do. After an exhausting race, they could have disastrous effects (such as stomach ache, including colic, diarrhea, and circulation problems).

I wish you lots of luck in your starts and hope you always enjoy yourself. There are so many serious things in life that in our free time, happiness and pleasure should come first.

You have made it to the finish line; now it is time to recover.

Nutrition

As a result of technical inno-
vations and the shortening of the
workweek, the physical demands
placed onto our bodies by our work
are continually decreasing. However,
most people have not adjusted their
nutrition to meet their body's altered
requirements. They eat as if they did
hard physical work, and often they
eat the wrong things. Their foods
are too rich in fats, contain too little
fiber, and have too many calories.
All natural foods contain different
percentages and combinations of
the same basic elements, namely
carbohydrates, fats, proteins, vitamins, minerals, trace elements, and
water. Pure fat or sugar crystals do
not occur naturally in isolation, and
they provide so-called empty calories. Empty for the simple reason that

a lot of ingredients have been
removed in the food preparation
process (as with white flour and
white rice). All that is left is the
energy-producing carbohydrates
and fat.

Unfortunately, consumption of
such snack foods is increasing, and
that produces a chain reaction. The
deficient nutrition leads to deficiencies of vitally important substances
such as vitamins and minerals in the
body. The body tries to signal its
deficit by means of increased
appetite. More food necessarily
entails an excess of calories, with
accompanying fat deposits and
overweight.

The same applies to alcohol,
from which most people nowadays
get about 10 percent of their caloric
needs. These too are empty calories.
In addition, alcohol damages cells,
especially in the liver. It has a further
disadvantage to athletes in that it
removes lots of fluid from the body

Relationship between nutritional groups and food groups (based on Hamm).

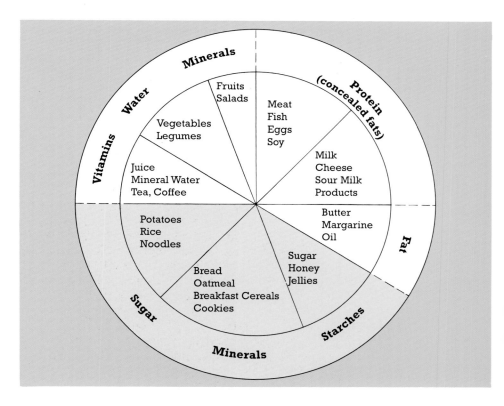

(producing an after-thirst). As a result, people should be aware of their daily need for calories based on their activity level. In addition, these calories must be provided through proper (that is, nutritionally valuable) foods.

The calorie is a unit of measurement from the science of heat. It can be understood simply as the amount of heat required to increase the temperature of one gram of water by one degree Centigrade. In 1978, the Joule was adopted worldwide as the unit of measurement for energy, work, and amount of heat. One calorie corresponds to about 4.2 Joules. A person's daily requirement is measured in kilocalories (one kcal = 1,000 calories) or in kilojoules. The amount depends on sex, age, and activity,as well as other factors, such as temperature and humidity. In addition, individual utilization of nutrition in the body needs to be considered. Nutritional plans must always be done on an individual basis. For all the importance that healthy, appropriate nutrition has for everyone, including athletes, the most important factors for athletic performance are still talent and training. Then comes nutrition. It is surely an exaggeration to turn food into an ideological pursuit. Even though the criticism of some trendy or fashionable nutrition practices is justified, there are still many very different and correct ways to eat properly.

The following ground rules can serve as a point of reference:
- ☐ Choose a variety of healthy foods that contain as many valuable nutritional elements as possible.
- ☐ Avoid consuming more calories than you need to maintain your weight.
- ☐ Avoid excess fats and cholesterol; take in more unsaturated fatty acids.
- ☐ Take in foods rich in fiber (except on race day).
- ☐ Reduce amounts of sugar taken in.
- ☐ Do not use much salt.
- ☐ Take in plenty of fluids (except alcohol).
- ☐ Consume as many unprocessed foods as possible.

Basic Nutritional Components

Carbohydrates

On a molecular level, carbohydrates are made up of the so-called simple sugars (monosaccharides), the best known of which are grape sugar (glucose) and fruit sugar (fructose). Two simple sugars join to form a complex sugar (disaccharide). That is how cane sugar and beet sugar (saccharose), malt sugar (maltose), and milk sugar (lactose) are formed. These couplings can be carried out to any length to yield oligosaccharides (involving three to ten simple sugars) and polysaccharides that can involve hundreds of thousands of basic building blocks (i.e., glucose molecules). They are found as cellulose or starches in the plant world. In humans and animals, the corresponding stored form of glucose is called glycogen.

115

Glucose is the most important energy dispenser in the human body. When glucose is burned, energy is released very quickly—much faster, for example, than when fat is broken down. In addition, the effectiveness of carbohydrate combustion is the greatest. That is, the breakdown of glucose releases more energy than is possible with the same amount of fat or protein. That is why the body first has recourse to carbohydrates and only later to the other energy stores. The presence of carbohydrates in the blood (at levels of 80 to 120 milligrams of glucose per 100 milliliters of blood) has to be kept fairly constant through a combination of usage and release since the nervous system, for example, is furnished with a constant supply of glucose. If the blood sugar decreases, a life-threatening situation may result. It is characterized by dizziness, spots in front of the eyes, the shakes, weakness, cold sweats, and other symptoms, and it is known as hypoglycemia.

The most important glycogen reservoirs in the human body are the liver and the muscles. Endurance training significantly increases the storage in the muscles by a factor of two or three.

For athletes, carbohydrates serve as the main energy source under workload. They last from eight seconds to about 40 minutes. Glucose can be burned aerobically in the presence of oxygen or broken down anaerobically in conditions of oxygen deficiency. In the first case, the only by-products are water and carbon dioxide (H_2O and CO_2), which can be completely and easily eliminated from the body. In the case of anaerobic energy production, lactic (milk) acid accumulates in the body. At certain levels, it interferes with cellular functions and limits performance (lactic acid buildup).

Carbohydrates are found in our foods primarily in grain products, potatoes, fruits, vegetables, and sweets. For reasons of healthy nutrition, natural, unprocessed foods (whole grain breads and rice, raw vegetables, salads, and fruit) are preferable to highly processed foods such as white flour, white sugar, and polished rice.

Fats and Lipids

Fat-soluble substances of widely varied chemical composition belong in this category, which perform a number of duties in the body. Among other functions, they store energy and provide heat insulation, a protective layer around the kidneys, and so-called organ fat in such places as the central nervous system. They also play an essential role in the functioning of hormones, vitamins (A, D, E, and K), and digestion (especially involving the liver and gallbladder).

The so-called neutral fats consist of glycerin, in which three fatty acids are combined. It is usual to speak of short-, medium-, and long-chain fatty acids as well as saturated and unsaturated fatty acids, depending on their chemical structure. The latter, like vitamins, are largely irreplaceable components of human nutrition since the body needs them and cannot produce them.

Runners depend increasingly on combustion of fatty acids to produce energy when they run for more than 40 minutes. Efficient breakdown of fatty acids fostered by training helps in the initial stages of long races and saves the limited carbohydrates that are available. Furthermore, polyunsaturated fatty acids provide protection against arteriosclerosis (restriction of the blood vessels). Fats also carry taste substances. Food with inadequate fat content is therefore not tolerable over the long term. Fats in the diet also involve some dangers, though. Cholesterol, which is a very important component of membranes and a preliminary stage of various active substances in the body, can entail arteriosclerosis and risk of heart attack. A high percentage of fat in the diet can foster intestinal cancer and interfere with the endurance that runners need.

The significance of this for our food choices is that fats should not exceed 25 percent of our overall food intake. Foods that contain cholesterol and fats (egg yolks, powdered eggs and milk, and animal fats) should not be included too frequently on the menu. Plant fats are preferable to animal fats, and we need to take in an adequate amount of free fatty acids.

Proteins

Proteins are the basic building blocks of all living material (*protos* comes from the Greek meaning first). On the molecular level, they are composed primarily of amino acids, some of which (the essential amino acids) must be taken in with foods. Others (the nonessential amino acids) can be synthesized or manufactured in the body.

There are a multitude of proteins in every cell, both in the form of structural elements and as enzymes that regulate entire biochemical processes. Proteins perform special tasks in the muscles (contraction), as the red blood substance hemoglobin (oxygen transport), and as carriers for nutritional substances and metabolic products. Proteins are also the framework for skin, hair, bones, and tendons. Additionally, they are responsible for defending the body against infection (by means of white blood cells, among others).

Our foods include plant and animal proteins, which on the basis of their biological valence can be classified as of greater or lesser importance to the human body. The following combinations of foods are particularly valuable for that reason: potatoes and eggs or milk and wheat, and corn and beans.

Strength athletes need lots of high-quality protein to foster muscular development. According to recent discoveries, even endurance athletes have an increased need for protein. In order to reach peak fitness and promote all vital functions, total protein in the diet should amount to 15 to 20 percent of food intake.

Foods consumed after strenuous exercise should contain plenty of the recovery-promoting amino acids valine, leucine, and arginine, which play an important role in neutralizing ammonia. The immune-system stimulant glutamine helps in reducing white blood corpuscles (B lymphocytes). Whey protein is particularly rich in the elements mentioned above.

Vitamins

Vitamins are substances that our body cannot manufacture for itself but which are vitally important to the functioning of many metabolic processes. They are sometimes referred to as biocatalysts. As a result, they must be taken in with foods. An athlete's need can be three or four times higher than normal, depending on how extensive and strenuous the training program is. It is important to know that certain vitamins (B_1, B_2, and C) are lost with sweat.

We distinguish between fat- and water-soluble vitamins. The latter include the entire B complex, C, folic acid, and niacin. Excessive amounts, for example in the form of high-dosage multivitamin tablets, are excreted by the kidneys. The case is different with the fat-soluble

117

vitamins, that is E, D, K, and A. When taken in excess, they are stored in fatty structures in the body (fatty tissues and nerve centers). Overdoses may uncommonly lead to symptoms of illness. In normal cases, we should get enough vitamins from a varied and nutritious diet. Just the same, the need for vitamins is surely higher in an athlete who trains regularly.

Antioxidants

Why do serious illnesses such as cancer occur in people who do not smoke, who abstain from alcohol, take no drugs, are neither overweight nor saddled with any other risk factors, and who regularly practice endurance training to keep fit? Scientists have examined this troublesome phenomenon and have stumbled onto the unexpected side effects of the *oxygen drug*.

An endurance athlete's body handles much more oxygen than that of a nonathlete. Under an intense athletic workload, the need for oxygen in body tissue can easily reach ten to 20 times the normal demand. In such cases, oxygen does not produce only positive effects. Specifically, it introduces a great number of what is known as free radicals. These substances are harmful to cells and can accelerate aging processes and

cause arteriosclerosis (constriction of blood vessels preparatory to a heart attack) plus a number of other illnesses.

These free radicals counteract substances known as antioxidants. The important antioxidants are the water-soluble vitamin C and fat-soluble vitamins E and beta-carotene. Selenium also works as a building block for an important enzyme. Specific information about doses of antioxidants has changed significantly in recent years. Now it is believed that fairly large amounts of antioxidants are necessary to the development of adequate immune defenses, particularly in athletes.

Recommended Daily Intake

Vitamin E	800 I.U.
Vitamin C	Men 2,000–4,000 mg
	Women 1,000–2,000 mg
Beta-carotene	5–10 mg
Selenium	100–200 mg

Minerals and Trace Elements

The fluids and tissues in the human body display a characteristic and constant amount of electrolytes (electrically charged, dissolved particles) that are known as isotones. There is a close relationship between water and

Oxygen Radicals, Metabolites, and Antioxidants

Free Radicals and Metabolites	Antioxidants
Peroxide radical ROO˙	Vitamin E
Oxygen $1O_2$	Beta-carotene Vitamins C and E
Superoxide O_2-˙	Superoxide dismutase
Hydroxyl radical OH˙	SH-group (amino acids)
Hydrogen peroxide H_2O_2	Glutathione peroxidase (selenium) Catalase

Water-Soluble Vitamins

Name	Source	Significance
Vitamin B$_1$ (thiamine)	Wheat germ, oatmeal, yeast, whole-grain products, pork, legumes	Carbohydrate metabolism, antioxidizing agent
Vitamin B$_2$ (riboflavin)	Milk, meat, grains, yeast, wheat germ	Energy production at the cellular level
Vitamin B$_6$ (pyridoxine)	Grains, meat, liver, yeast, fish	Protein metabolism, antioxidizing agent
Vitamin B$_{12}$ (cobalamin)	All animal-based foods	Forming red corpuscles
Vitamin C (ascorbic acid)	Fresh fruit and vegetables (citrus fruits, rose hips, potatoes, paprika, nettle)	Forming connective tissue, antioxidizing agent
Folic acid	Green leafy vegetables, wheat germ, liver, yeast	Amino acid metabolism
Pantothenic acid	Widespread in plant- and animal-based foods	Antioxidizing agent
Niacin	Pork, yeast, whole-grain products, potatoes	Energy production at cellular level
Biotin	Soy flour, liver, yeast (also produced by intestinal bacteria)	Enzyme component

Fat-Soluble Vitamins

Name	Source	Significance
Vitamin A (retinol)	Liver, cod liver oil, milk products, egg yolk	Vision, skin and mucous membranes, growth
Provitamin A (beta-carotene)	Carrots, paprika, tomatoes, apricots, lettuce, green cabbage, etc.	Vision, skin and mucous membranes, growth
Vitamin D	Liver, cod liver oil, egg yolk; is manufactured in human skin in the presence of sunshine	Calcium metabolism—builds bones
Vitamin E	Wheat germ, whole-grain products, eggs, plant oils, natural rice, vegetables	Fat metabolism (antioxidizing agent
Vitamin K	In many foods; can be produced by intestinal bacteria	Blood coagulation

electrolytes in maintaining a balance. The most important functions of minerals are in transferring impulses in nerves and muscles, maintaining electric stability in cell membranes, and providing a specific osmotic pressure (*osmos* from the Greek meaning impetus; the force needed to maintain a constant fluid level in cells and blood vessels).

Sodium, potassium, calcium, and magnesium, plus chloride, phosphate, and bicarbonate, are the most important electrolytes. Iron, zinc, manganese, copper, iodine, and selenium are the most important trace elements.

Sodium and chloride are found as table salt in nearly all foods. Sodium is also retained from sweat and conserved by the body. A true lack of sodium is therefore possible only under extreme conditions, such as in a marathon run in humid weather.

Sources and significance of the most important minerals.

Minerals

Name	Source	Significance
Sodium (Na)	Table salt, salted and smoked foods	Osmotic pressure in extra-cellular space, bioelectrical system, enzyme functions
Potassium (K)	Widespread in plant-based foods	Osmotic pressure inside cells, bioelectrical system, enzyme functions
Chloride (Cl)	Table salt, salted and smoked foods	Osmotic pressure in extra-cellular space, stomach acids
Calcium (Ca)	Milk, milk products, vegetables, fruits, grains	Bone structure, neuromuscular sensitivity, muscle contraction, blood coagulation
Magnesium (Mg)	Wheat germ, legumes, fowl, fish, vegetables, fruit	Bone structure, enzyme function, muscle functioning
Phosphorus (P)	Milk, meat, grains, fish, eggs	Bone structure, cell energy production, membrane functions

Iron, phosphorus, and magnesium, on the other hand, are lost in greater amounts with sweat and are extremely important for endurance athletes. A phosphorus deficiency is manifested in muscle weakness, fatigue, and inability to perform. A lack of magnesium can lead to muscle cramps. After fairly lengthy workloads, it can take days or even weeks to fill up the magnesium reservoirs in the body again.

Iron is especially important for endurance athletes since it is essential for oxygen and carbon dioxide transport. It also facilitates myoglobin's role in storing oxygen and plays a pivotal role in the cellular breathing chain. In athletes, there is an increased need in cases of

Trace Elements

Name	Source	Significance
Silicium	Bran, plant fibers	Bone structure, formation of connective tissue and cartilage
Zinc (Zn)	Green peas, cheese, eggs, meat, fish, liver, oranges	Growth, sexual functions, skin structure, healing, appetite
Iron (Fe)	Liver, beer hops, chives, whole-grain products, parsley, broccoli, red cabbage	Enzyme components, oxygen transport
Manganese (Mn)	Grains, spinach, berries, legumes	Bones and cartilage
Fluorine (F)	Meat, eggs, fruits, vegetables	Tooth and bone structure
Copper (Cu)	Legumes, liver, nuts	Elastic fibers (large blood vessels), bone structure, blood production
Iodine (I)	Eggs, milk, ocean fish	Thyroid function, physical and mental development
Selenium (Se)	Meat, fish, beer hops, whole-grain products, fruits, vegetables	Antioxidizing agent, muscle function, blood coagulation

heightened excretion of sweat, urine, stool, and a significant decrease in red blood corpuscles (hemolysis). In an independent study of 50 female runners, it was found that 29 of them experienced an iron deficiency, as compared with only two of 50 female nonathletes. Often what you take in with foods is not enough to offset a deficiency. Since it is not a good idea to take iron pills as a preventive measure without a doctor's supervision and taking mineral tablets over a long term is not for everyone, you can first try to meet the heightened need by consuming such things as hops, dried fruits, wheat germ, and cocoa drinks. It is a good idea for female runners to have their levels of iron, ferritin, and hemoglobin checked regularly—perhaps quarterly.

Further trace elements that are important for the human body, but whose significance has not yet been completely explained by research, include molybdenum, arsenic, cobalt, nickel, chromium, tin, vanadium, rubidium, and cesium.

Fluids (Water)

Fluids are at least as important as the solid components of human nutrition. The human body consists of 57 to 70 percent water. It serves as a solvent, an energy conveyor, and a building material. It contributes to chemical reactions and helps keep the body temperature at an even level. The body temperature rises with as little as a 2 percent loss by body weight of fluid. With a 5 percent loss, heart rate increases and oxygen transport is disrupted. A person may not survive a water loss of just 10 percent. A well-trained athlete can produce up to 2 to 3 quarts/liters of sweat per hour. This calls for a timely and adequate intake of fluids during training and competition.

■ Nutrition for Endurance Athletes

Nutrition in the Training Phase

The human body has adapted to the rhythmic changes of nature over the course of millions of years. Seasons, phases of the moon, and the continuum of night and day trigger responses in regulatory processes that we do not yet understand fully. However, such things as hormone release are subject to the circadian 24-hour rhythm, and that influences our appetite, need for sleep, and other bodily functions.

We should take these fluctuations into account and plan our nutritional intake and mealtimes accordingly.

It is a good idea to eat at the same time every day. We should take in 30 to 40 percent of our caloric requirements in the morning, 20 to 25 percent at midday, another 15 percent in the afternoon, and 20 to 25 percent in the evening.

To enhance the digestibility of food, you should observe a couple of basic rules, which of course apply also to nonathletes:
- ☐ Chew your food well to help digestion.
- ☐ Choose foods low in fat.
- ☐ Restrict animal-based foods.
- ☐ Avoid concentrated sweets.
- ☐ Avoid very cold or very hot foods and drinks.

Ideally, training should be done at the same time each day. In warm, humid, unfamiliar weather

121

conditions, people who live in latitudes such as ours are advised to take in adequate fluids in a timely fashion. Athletes who drink more sweat less than those who attempt to suppress their thirst. In the former, the well-filled blood vessels emit more heat and need to produce less sweat to regulate body temperature. So the old axiom about good athletes not drinking much applies only to alcoholic drinks. It is also true that the ability to sweat copiously when the body becomes overheated is a protective measure that can save a person's life. (For information about heat prostration, see page 144.) A beneficial drink that also contains important vitamins and minerals is apple or grape juice mixed in equal proportions with mineral water.

A significant effect of endurance training is an increase in glycogen reserves of up to two to three times. This helps keep the body supplied for as long as possible with valuable and economical energy from carbohydrates. You should also realize that after emptying the reserves, about 48 hours are required to fill them up again. The first ten hours are particularly important; they are known as the *quick phase* of the rebuilding process. So shortly after a hard workout or a race, you should have a sumptuous meal of carbohydrates (such as pasta, rice, potatoes, vegetables, fruits, and cereals) along with plenty to drink. You should also be sure that the foods contain lots of potassium (such as dried fruits, bananas, nuts, wheat germ, and bouillon from meat extract) since potassium and water are required for rebuilding glycogen reserves.

Charts that illustrate the total calories that the body needs can be useful in comparing your dietary habits with an ideal. However, as athletes deal with their body in the course of a training year, they develop a natural feel for how it

Blood sugar levels with and without carbohydrate intake in a 90-minute workout at about 70 percent maximum intensity.

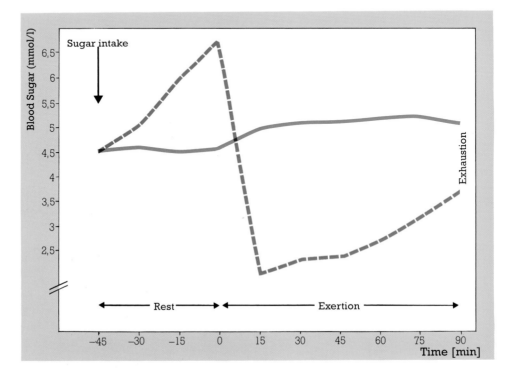

Average Amount of Time Various Foods Remain in the Stomach

6 to 8 hours	Sardines, roast goose, stews, sauerkraut, cabbage
5 to 6 hours	Bacon, smoked salmon, tuna fish, pickles, mushrooms, French fries and other fried food, roast pork, chops
4 to 5 hours	Roast beef, baked fish, steak, pork cutlets, peas, lentils, white and green beans, cream torte
3 to 4 hours	Dark bread, cheese, raw fruit, green lettuce, stewed vegetables, chicken filets, ham, grilled veal, fried potatoes, baked goods
2 to 3 hours	Lean meat, cooked vegetables, boiled potatoes, cooked pasta, scrambled eggs, omelets, bananas, steak tartar
1 to 2 hours	Milk, yogurt, cocoa, low-fat cheese, white bread, soft-boiled eggs, mashed potatoes, rice
1 hour	Tea, coffee, buttermilk, skim milk, reduced-fat bouillon
1/2 hour	Small amounts of glucose, fructose, honey, isotonic electrolyte drinks, alcohol

reacts to workloads and for its caloric needs. That is why most top-level athletes maintain a constant body weight even without checking it. In the winter, it is usually 2 to 5 pounds (1 to 2 kg) higher than in the summer. However, people who need objective information should regularly check their body weight after getting up in the morning and before eating. It is even more valuable in the long run to keep track of the body's fat composition. The impedance method is easy to perform and has proven reliable.

Nutrition in the Competition Phase

Runners should be sure to take in a particularly high quantity of carbohydrates in the last days before an important race. The Swedish diet, which some people used to follow, is hardly used any more. This involved emptying the carbohydrate reserves by following a fat and protein diet in combination with strenuous endurance training up to three or four days before the race and then eating a very high carbohydrate diet to fill up the glycogen depots above normal levels. The calculated

drop-off in performance a few days before the competition is simply too difficult for most people to cope with.

It is equally important to get adequate amounts of minerals (K, Mg, and Fe) and vitamins (C, B complex, and E) so you do not report to the race with a deficit.

In addition, the body should be supplied with adequate amounts of water right up to shortly before starting time (30 minutes to an hour). A hypotonic or very thin carbohydrate solution is reabsorbed most quickly, even faster than pure water. It is a good idea to add a small amount of soluble crystals to the above-mentioned mixture of apple or grape juice and uncarbonated mineral water in a one-to-one ratio. Coffee and tea have also been proven to be stimulating and useful drinks. When two to three cups are consumed before a competition, they slightly enhance physical and mental performance and simultaneously encourage combustion of fat. This spares the carbohydrate reserves in the initial stages of a race.

The last solid meal should be two or three hours before starting time (fours hours is even better) so that the food is no longer in the stomach. The meal should consist

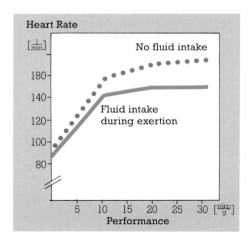

Illustration of the effect of fluid intake on heart rate at high outside temperatures and various levels of exertion. At high outside temperatures, the heart rate (and the work that the heart has to perform) can be reduced by regular intake of fluids.

of carbohydrates that are easy to digest (pasta, rice, and potatoes, for example) and very little fat, protein, and—contrary to the usual recommendation—fiber, and it should not be too sumptuous. The body needs about an hour and a half to accomplish most of the digestion for that type of meal. At this point in time, it is a good idea to rest up physically and mentally.

It is not advisable to take in concentrated carbohydrate drinks in the last hours before the race. The body will react to the short-term increase in blood sugar by releasing additional insulin. This leads to a significant decrease in blood sugar level at the wrong time during competition. A massive period of relative weakness (*the bonk*) is the unavoidable result, and it is the exact opposite of the original intent.

Nutrition During the Race

For races lasting up to about 45 minutes, there is usually no need for nutritional intake. The energy storehouses in a well-trained human body are adequate for such workloads. However, if the race is longer than that, such as a marathon, runners should start early to take in fluids— long before they feel thirst or a decrease in performance signals a deficiency. It is best to take small

sips, ideally starting at the 3-mile (5-km) point. Fairly recent studies show that cold drinks can be taken in since they are quicker to leave the stomach and they help keep the body temperature low in hot weather. The important thing is to avoid creating stomach problems. The previously mentioned mixed prerace drink is recommended as long it is possible to use it in a given event. The body's ability to take in significant quantities of food during a race is quite doubtful. Under intense workloads, the blood supply to the digestive system is reduced to a minimum. In any case, small amounts of carbohydrates seem to find their way to the right place—the muscles.

Nutrition After the Race

After a strenuous run, lost fluids first need to be replaced. The *competition mix* (see page 123) is a good choice. It is absorbed quickly, and it simultaneously supplies the body with fluid, carbohydrates for energy, and vitamins and minerals. But do not drink too much of it, or too fast, or too cold.

Perhaps an hour or two later, after the body has rested up, you can have a meal rich in carbohydrates and protein (see pages 115 and 117) to replenish the empty reserves.

Women and Running

■ Some History

Investigations into the history of women's sports lead to some astonishing revelations. Nowadays, the fact that women are turning in excellent times at the same distances as men represents sensational progress. As recently as 1968 at the Mexico City Olympic Games, the longest women's race was 800 meters because people felt that women had to be protected from the dangers that longer races would present to their bodies.

In ancient times, the Spartans subjected girls to the same physical discipline as boys. That included long-distance races, where in many schools girls competed directly with the boys.

Practically all modern discoveries about endurance sports for women were familiar to the ancient Greeks. People back then already knew that "a strong body carries inside it the seed of healthy development," and "strong women endure birthing better than women who are not physically fit." Plato even advocated regular exercise for pregnant women so that the fetus could experience a little exercise.

However, the social position of women changed as the centuries went on. Up to the end of the nineteenth century, sports in our culture were considered strictly the affair of men. In the Middle Ages, women were regarded as fragile beings unfit for sports. In other cultures, women were subjected to physical labor but for other reasons, there were no women athletes.

Hassiba Boulmerka (Algeria, wearing number 53), whose 1,500-meter victory at the 1992 Olympic Games in Barcelona created waves in the sports world far beyond her homeland.

127

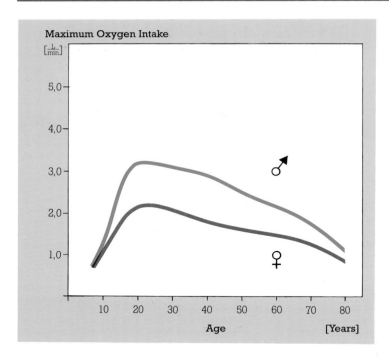

Maximum Oxygen Intake

$[\frac{l}{min}]$

Maximum oxygen intake over the lifetime of men and women as an indication of performance.

runners. However, we created a different set of experiences for them with their efforts to gain recognition in this century. We can recall the statement of a formerly well-known athlete after middle-distance races were instituted for women when he remarked that "Now that women have a 1,500-meter event, we'll just not watch for five minutes." Nowadays, the marathon has become a given for women. It has been proven that long-distance running ability is not sex specific, but depends more on a person's talent.

Performance Medicine

The average physical build of a woman is first distinguished from that of a man by lesser body weight and a higher percentage of body fat. Women have less muscle in proportion to overall body weight (around 25 to 30 percent) than do men (about 40 to 50 percent).

With respect to the (passive) musculoskeletal system, women have a lighter skeletal structure and less tight connective tissue. Their muscles are more flexible than men's. This means that their spine is more susceptible to strains due to repetitive stress. These types of injuries can be prevented by muscle strengthening and back exercises. Otherwise, women have no disadvantages with their musculoskeletal system in comparison with men.

The circulatory system of women shows a reduced capacity for oxygen transport, even considering the differences in body weight. The volume of their heart and lungs is smaller, their blood pressure is lower, and they have less hemoglobin (red blood cells). The main reason for this is that since men have greater muscle mass,

Until modern times, there was a strictly prescribed role for women in many parts of the world. Especially given the usual marriageable age of 16, it was out of the question for them to continue to engage in sports. Their duty has been to bear children and care for them, the husband, and the household. If it were not for that, we might expect to see an equally high number of women runners from Africa at the top of the field in long-distance races alongside the outstanding African male runners.

In the industrialized nations, women have taken the plunge and demonstrated that they were not excluded from sports for centuries because of a lack of natural ability but, rather, because of societal prejudices. However, it was still a long road for female athletes to today's understanding, and prejudice and abuse accompanied them on the way. In running events, women had to struggle race by race. The poets of antiquity saw beauty in female

Who says distance running makes women unattractive? Elana Meyer (Republic of South Africa) was one of the world's best long-distance runners in the 1990s.

Women's races (like this one in Bern, Switzerland—one of Europe's largest) are an expression of women's new self-confidence, and not just in sports.

they have a greater need for oxygen. In sitting, standing, and walking, men need about 10 percent more oxygen than women do.

On the other hand, heart and circulatory system training works just as well for both sexes. With the right type of training, a woman can make the same type of relative progress that a man can. A comparable enlargement of the heart muscle produces in women an even greater reduction in the resting heart rate than in men; in other words, women develop a greater economy of heart rate. Even though there are limits to the strength that women can develop, that seems to apply less to endurance. Among all the types of sports in which women have traditionally excelled, we can now add long-distance running. Since 1985, the world record in the marathon has been a previously unimaginable 2:21:06. When the Norwegian runner Ingrid Kristiansen sprinted for the finish in the effort that yielded this record in London, she looked amazingly fresh. She has proven (as have

Grete Waitz, Joan Benoit, Ute Pippig, and Katrin Dörre, among others) that a woman can train as hard as a man. That is true for the number of miles per week and the relative intensity of the training.

■ Training for Women

As already described in the chapter about training (see pages 35ff. and 61ff.), purpose, goal setting, and an investment of time in running vary greatly among individuals. For a beginner, it is a good idea to alternate walking and running until it is possible to jog at a comfortable pace without interruption for about a half hour. Two to three times a week is enough to get the body slowly used to the increased workload. The heart and circulatory system and the musculoskeletal system need time to adjust gradually. This process can be complemented by regular strength and flexibility exercises. Injuries can be prevented especially by doing exercises to strengthen the back, gluteals, stomach muscles, and the muscles of the foot and lower leg (see pages 86 to 91); this will also hasten progress in running.

Purely for reasons of health, three workouts per week consisting of 40 minutes of distance running (and do not forget the previously mentioned warm-up exercises!) should be enough at first; after that, there are not any upper limits. Experience shows that most people are not content to stick with that type of program. Once the bug bites, people generally want more. There are some stimulating races that are worth training for and that may turn into unforgettable experiences (see page 105). This wave will carry you out of the realm of mere fitness sports into performance-oriented athletics.

Maximum dynamic strength development of school-age boys and girls using the example of bench presses.

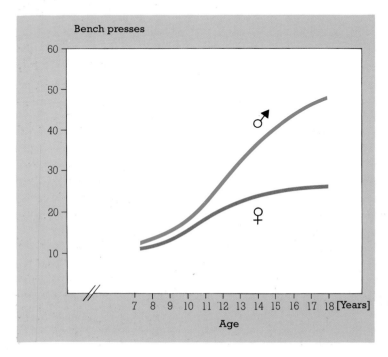

Bench presses

In this second phase, you should vary your running speed and broaden your range of training. Speed play and hill running (see page 44) offer variety and effectiveness, especially to the extent that strength and stretching exercises are included as a permanent part of training.

The step up to competitive running is now a good deal easier, and a little talent and dedication will pay dividends on the training. For women, the field is not as crowded as it is for men. For a long time, there has been room for advancement. You do not really need to do two workouts a day, as the top women runners in the world do. Adequate, intensive training on a daily basis will still win a number of national-class races.

■ Health

People usually realize how important health is when they are sick or do not feel well. Wise people plan ahead for such eventualities. The many people who run regularly already know that "Running makes you fit" is more than a catchy slogan. Oftentimes, the motivation to get started with training is tied to a desire to shed a few pounds. Fortunately, this result is not long in arriving. Suddenly, you fit back into an earlier clothing size since you have trimmed down your waistline, and you can sleep deeply and soundly. In short, you feel several years younger, and outward appearance is an important factor for a women's self-confidence.

On the subject of sports and cancer, not long ago a scientific study was done on American women. In all, nearly 5,500 women were examined. About half of them participated regularly in sports and the other half not at all. It was found that the athletic women had a risk two to two-and-a-half times smaller of contracting cancer of the reproductive organs. A possible reason for this difference was the enhanced circulation to the organs and the improved oxygen supply they received as well as general activation of the immune system (defense against illness-causing pathogens and recognizing and destroying sick cells in the body) in the case of female runners. In addition, hormonal causes evidently played a role through reduced body fat and lower estrogen levels.

Based on anatomic and physiological factors, women are more susceptible to hypothermia, which may cause discomfort in menstruation. Intense effort in cold and wet weather may present a danger of gynecological and urinary tract inflammation. It is a good idea to dress appropriately and wear a pair of light tights (see page 29) in a race rather than risk an infection.

It is normal for many women to feel less energetic on some days than on others. Beginning runners always ask if they should run during their period. On medical grounds there should be no misgivings. Menstruation is a natural process in women's bodies and not some kind of illness. It should therefore also have no negative impact on performance. Most women experience a peak in their performance directly after their period and a slight low immediately before. Investigations during the Tokyo Olympics revealed that the medal winners were at widely varied stages of their menstrual cycles. Normally, it is not advisable to postpone one's period through medication because of a race. On the other hand, problems that may crop up at this time may be avoided or reduced by cutting back a little on training. Often, the cramps that accompany the menstrual cycle can be made to disappear altogether, or at least be made more bearable, with some light jogging. Some side effects such as back- or headaches and general fatigue can be improved, plus depression can be eliminated and the blood flow can be shortened.

In many highly competitive women athletes, long-term strenuous training can produce irregularities in menstruation (oligomenorrhea), and menstruation may disappear entirely (amenorrhea). The latter can also be triggered by psychological stress such as test anxiety and professional and family difficulties.

Control centers in the brain regulate hormone production, especially involving LH (the luteotropic hormone) and estrogen (the female sex hormone). The layer of subcutaneous fat decreases with training, and there are some changes in mineral balances (such as with calcium). These may be restored if training is cut back. There is usually no danger of anything more than temporary functional disorders;

they usually have no effect on a woman's health or recuperative powers. The situation may be different, though, when a young girl gets involved in competitive sports before the onset of puberty. The heart and circulatory system may grow to handle the premature, strenuous training, but that is not the case with the hormone control mechanisms and the musculoskeletal system. The first menstruation (menarche) is prepared by an irregular release of LH from the pituitary gland. Intensive training can suppress this mechanism and produce a major delay in the onset of menstruation. Very common effects later on include menstrual irregularities and even calcium deficiencies in the bones (osteoporosis).

Another weak point in the young body is the musculoskeletal system. Before growth is complete, the

It is always a good idea for women to wear warm clothing in cold weather.

133

growth joints are the areas of highest metabolic activity. Consequently, they are very sensitive to stress. The greatest danger is to upper and lower vertebrae, muscles, and tendons, such as at the head of the shinbone.

Because of the monthly blood loss, women frequently suffer from iron deficiency. As we have already pointed out in the chapter on nutrition (see page 114), iron is necessary for production of red blood cells, which function as oxygen carriers in the blood. In addition, oxygen plays an essential role in energy production and therefore has a decisive effect on performance. It is a good idea for women to have their blood tested regularly and, if necessary, to take over an extended period of time iron supplements recommended by a doctor.

There is another special women's problem that is seldom discussed for reasons of modesty but which is quite common in older women. In long runs or in jumping, urine is released from the bladder even though it has just been emptied. A reason for this can be a uterus that is sagging with age and a reduction in the ability to seal off the bladder. As far as we know, this inconvenience cannot be eliminated, but it can be reduced by exercises that strengthen the abdominal muscles in the lower part of the pelvis.

Here is an example: Lie flat on your back and place your feet onto the floor. Arms lie on either side next to the body. Now lift your bottom, and squeeze your bottom muscles together as hard as you can. Breathe out as you do this. Hold this position for a few seconds, then relax again by lowering your bottom to the floor and breathing in. You should do this exercise in sets of 20 repetitions. (See page 161 for one-legged execution.)

Pregnancy

The first pregnancy is a really sensational experience in a woman's life. A woman who's accustomed to regular training can continue with moderate running as long as she is comfortable. A basic requirement for that is a normal pregnancy. There must also be no predisposition to miscarriage. Women should be especially careful in the eighth, twelfth, and sixteenth weeks after their last period and avoid rough shaking (such as jumping exercises). At these times, there may be a heightened sensitivity in the uterus that could conceivably lead to a miscarriage.

When you are pregnant, the main thing in training is to pay attention to how you feel and not try to compete with other women. Even in the same woman, different pregnancies can be very different in nature. In addition, you should keep up some regular exercise. That makes delivery easier, and the body will get back into shape quicker afterward. All exercises that strengthen the back and stomach muscles are appropriate, as are breathing exercises.

Many women feel forced to lay off running, when they become pregnant. In the first years of their offspring's life the combination of child care, work, and family is new and difficult, which also keeps them from running.

The Baby Jogger can help solve this problem. It allows the running mother to take the child along and help the youngster grow to like running. Critical points include a compromised sitting position and poor shock absorption. However, the Baby Jogger is a very good compromise for fairly short workouts on smooth, paved courses. It allows young mothers to improve their fitness with a clear conscience since the little one is part of the activity.

Clothing— Attractive and Practical

Basically, what we said on pages 24 through 32 applies to clothing. Today people can dress practically and attractively. The clothing industry has come up with a tremendous selection in recent years.

There are just two footnotes especially for women: many women runners have trouble wearing their bra in training. They should purchase a sports bra.

The other body part that women should protect is the lower abdomen. For extra warmth, knee-length wool underwear can be worn.

Training with a Baby Jogger.

Sports Medicine

Endurance Training— Preventing Heart and Circulatory Disease

In recent years, statistics have shown that a very significant number of deaths are the result of diseases of the heart and circulatory system. Surprisingly, slightly more than half of those victims are women, a fact explainable by the asymmetrical shape of the age pyramid.

Doctors and scientists have determined the essential importance of inadequate exercise among the risk factors currently recognized. There are direct or indirect connections involving, on the one hand, lack of exercise and being overweight, and on the other, elevated blood sugar (diabetes mellitus), stress, high blood pressure (arterial hypertonia), elevated lipoproteins in the blood (hyperlipoproteinemia), excess uric acid in the blood (gout), and cigarette smoking. It is well known that involvement in athletics reduces weight more effectively than any diet fad (a 6.2 mile (10 km) run burns up about 700 calories). In addition, there are some beneficial changes in hormonal and psychological conditions. It has been proven that people who are in shape find it easier to eliminate harmful habits related to nutrition and snacking, including cigarette smoking.

The endurance sports of walking and jogging are the most important preventive measures against diseases of the heart and circulatory system . . .

Take diabetes for example: Regular endurance training lowers blood sugar levels, and more receptors for insulin are produced. On top of everything else, that helps curb the appetite.

The autonomic nervous system is subdued and fewer stress hormones (catecholamines) are produced. As a result, stressful situations can be tolerated better. Anxiety and uncertainty are replaced by composure and self-confidence.

These same mechanisms are also responsible for the mild effect that distance running has in lowering blood pressure. Additional effects include weight loss and reduced sodium content in the blood due to loss through sweating. The positive effects on uric acid levels in the blood are also known. Lipoprotein levels likewise show clear changes. The particularly harmful LDL substances (low-density lipoproteins) are greatly reduced, and the overall amount of fats in the blood decreases. HDL 2 (high-density lipoprotein), which has somewhat of a protective function, increases. If there were a medication that had these qualities (with no side effects!), it would surely sell like hotcakes.

The direct effects that endurance training has on the heart and circulatory system are well documented. The heightened effect of the parasympathetic nervous system (part of the autonomic nervous system) reduces heart rate, improves the efficiency of the contractions in the heart muscle (thereby saving energy), and lengthens distole (the heart's relaxation phase between two beats, during which the heart muscle is supplied with blood). Even in the outer reaches of the circulatory system there are signs of adaptation. In well-trained skeletal muscles, the storage capacities for oxygen (myoglobin) and carbohydrates (glycogen) are increased, and more enzymes are produced for energy- producing processes. Oxygen transport is facilitated by an increase in small blood vessels (capillaries) in the muscles. The resistance that the heart has to overcome in doing its work is reduced. In addition, there are improvements in the flow qualities of the blood, the formation of red blood cells (erythrocytes), and the stability of the blood platelets (thrombocytes) by way of thrombosis prevention (*thrombosis* from the Greek meaning blood clotting; formation of blockages in uninjured veins).

All these adaptations reduce the oxygen requirements of the heart muscle (under comparable load). In that way, the safety zone between oxygen supply and demand is expanded, and the probability of a heart attack is greatly reduced. In order to achieve these adaptations fully, training should be done three times a week for about 40 minutes each. A balanced, mild workload—that is, an aerobic one—is preferable to interval training because of its more positive effect on the autonomic nervous system.

The heart rate is the decisive factor in establishing the intensity of the training. The area between

130 and 160 beats per minute is a statistical boundary that defines an effective but essentially safe training effort. Precise determination of the best intensity for any individual is best accomplished through a lactose step test. That makes it possible to gauge the appropriate heart rate with a monitor. The previously feared enlarged heart produced by endurance sports has been proven by discoveries in sports medicine to be a normal adaptation of the heart muscle to the elevated demands placed on the circulatory system. The effect is quite similar to increasing the size of the biceps through strength training. Just as no one is forced to lift weights for an entire lifetime, endurance athletes are not condemned to run long into old age (however, they may do so if they feel like it). Similarly, since the heart muscle (and not the heart chambers, as with cardiac defects) is increased gradually, the hypertrophy diminishes to a certain extent when the level of training is cut back.

It is practically never too late to start training. The effects described above are observable into old age, even among people who begin sports for the first time in their 60s and 70s. That was determined by a series of experiments conducted at the German Sports Academy in Cologne.

Before taking up regular athletic training, it is always a good idea to have a complete and relevant medical checkup. At ages over 35, that should be considered mandatory. If the examination reveals any history of illness such as a cardiac defect, heartbeat irregularities, a previous heart attack, an existing infection, or other problems, sports should be practiced only under medical supervision, such as in a cardiac walking group. Modified training that stresses coordination, flexibility (agility), and strengthening and relaxation exercises can facilitate economical movements and muscle use, thereby reducing oxygen requirements and demands on the heart.

◼ Running and Age

Aging is a biological process that none of us can escape. The speed at which our ability to perform declines, however, is greatly subject to our actions. So some individuals can achieve major differences between their chronological and biological ages.

Numerous factors influence the loss of physical and mental abilities in old age. At first, muscle strength and muscle mass begin to decline (atrophy) much more quickly and drastically in the legs than in the arms. However, fat deposits increase for a while and then decline again in old age. Connective and protective tissues lose their flexibility, and joints subsequently lose theirs. Tendons and muscles are more easily

. . . and the right type of workload for the bodies of older people.

damaged by sudden workloads. Next are the functions of the endocrine glands, which are used for hormone production. The production of the male sex hormone testosterone, which is of great significance for muscle strength, reduces by about a third. Still later, the mental capacities decline, followed ultimately by the psychological functions such as thinking, the ability to concentrate, deep feeling, and coordination. Up to the age of 80, the brain loses about 20 percent of its maximum weight.

Illnesses can accelerate the aging processes but so can lack of exercise and training. The heart and circulatory system remain responsive to training long into old age. People in their 60s who engage in regular endurance training have been observed to have circulatory systems comparable to those of people 30 years younger who are not in shape. The natural age-related changes in the blood vessels—loss of elasticity—set in up to two decades later. The decrease in breathing functions (e.g., reduced vital capacity), which is observable starting as early as the midthirties, can be delayed significantly through endurance training. Even autonomic regulatory disorders such as sleeplessness, digestive problems, and heightened sensitivity to temperature can be prevented or at least reduced. There is also a positive psychological influence that manifests itself in increased self-confidence and joie de vivre. The responsiveness of skeletal muscles to training declines continually from about age 30. Loss of strength can be delayed by strength training. When given comparable effort though, the results at age 70 are only about a third of a person's previous maximum capacity.

Competing in sports into old age is not without its problems.

Anyway, the type of athletics should be adjusted to a person's age. Starting in the 50s and 60s, aerobic endurance training is by far the most sensible choice. Because tissues and blood vessels are less flexible, and since there is a greater susceptibility to irregular heartbeat (arrhythmia), it is a good idea to cut back on weight lifting and other explosive, maximum workloads such as sprints. At this age, high-performance competitive sports should also be gradually eliminated.

Recommended sports include dynamic and endurance-oriented ones such as distance running, cross-country skiing, bicycling, swimming (not in excessively cold water), hiking, and rowing. Noncompetitive tennis and game sports should be accompanied by endurance training workouts. Golf fosters muscle coordination.

No one can avoid growing older. Recent experiments have shown, though, that in male and female laboratory animals, regular, appropriate physical activity can increase life expectancy by up to 25 percent. Two independent research teams in the United States have determined that improving individual fitness likewise produces increased life expectancy among humans. Small amounts of fairly mild endurance training appear to make the body less sensitive to what is known as auto-oxidation—a process whereby substances lose their chemical and biochemical characteristics through uncontrolled reactions with oxygen radicals, as in the case of rusting iron. This process is thought to play an important role in the development of cancer and seems to accelerate the aging process through the accumulation of harmful metabolic products (see "Antioxidants," page 118).

Running and the Psyche

The more our surroundings become automated, especially at work, the more urgent it becomes to find meaningful and useful activities for our continually increasing free time. The more people elect to run or jog as the perfect way to counterbalance the demands of work, the louder the unavoidable, critical voices become: running is nothing but running away from the elusive problems of everyday life, and it is an addiction comparable to drug dependency.

In the face of such an antagonistic opinion, many people are motivated to tackle the subject on a scientific basis. As it turns out, they are not all of the same opinion. However, the investigations have produced some results that make it easier to understand some of the effects of running.

What is known as endorphins may be at least partially responsible for the psychological effects of running. This involves substances that are produced by the body and that in their chemical structure resemble the painkiller morphine. That helps explain their effect on human pain perception as well as on other sense perceptions, emotions, and moods. It is generally agreed today that athletic activity such as running fosters a sense of well-being that can last for several hours. Tension, worries, and anxiety are reduced, and a tendency to depression gives way to increased self-confidence and a positive outlook. Today's many autonomic disorders are ideally suited to running as a form of therapy. The purely physical effects of running have already been described in this chapter (see page 137). They result in a broad-based improvement in physical condition.

The World Health Organization (WHO) defines health as the greatest possible physical, mental, and social well-being. We have to understand that running is not a cure-all. To all appearances, regular running helps us get a good deal closer to this ideal. If we experience *withdrawal symptoms* after a couple of days without training and if this represents a certain dependency on an activity that gives us relaxation, happiness, and health, at least in contrast to the many other addictions that we are accused of nowadays (such as watching television, listening to rock music, overeating, consumerism, and so forth), this one certainly is not the worst.

Running with Existing Illnesses

Before you get started on a regular training program, even if you already participate in sports on a sporadic basis, it is a good idea to have an internal (and ideally an orthopedic) checkup. This should be considered mandatory for anyone over the age of 35. In Germany, trade associations, sports leagues, and the German Institute for Sports place so much emphasis on intensive medical care that they require semiannual checkups of their athletes.

A relaxing run: physical and mental regeneration for young and old.

Depending on the scope and intensity of their training, even recreational athletes should have a medical checkup every one to two years. The purpose of the internal checkup is to identify any preexisting illnesses, especially ones that would counterindicate regular endurance training. These include:

○ Congenital heart defects
○ Cardiac insufficiency (heart weakness), hereditary heart defect (e.g., inflammation of the heart muscle or membranes)
○ Constriction of blood vessels (arteriosclerosis), with frequent heart problems, especially at rest
○ Significant abnormalities in heart rhythm
○ Aneurysms or bulges in the wall of the heart or blood vessels
○ Harmful enlargement of the heart
○ Unresponsive heartbeat
○ Condition after recent heart attack
○ Condition after bleeding in the esophagus, acute stomach, or intestinal ulcer
○ Recent embolism
○ Acute inflammation of veins (thrombophlebitis)
○ Acute, feverish infectious diseases
○ Other serious general illnesses such as tumors or nerve problems
○ Serious types of high blood pressure
○ Metabolic deficiencies such as diabetes mellitus, immune deficiencies
○ Ergometer performance under 75 watts

In such cases, participation in sports may aggravate the illness.

On the other hand, there are numerous types of internal diseases that can be helped by regular, mild endurance training. For example, with chronic lung diseases such as bronchial asthma and emphysema, the remaining function can be utilized more efficiently. Breathing becomes more economical, the breathing rhythm improves,

143

breathing muscles are strengthened, and the oxygen that is taken into the body can be used more effectively.

People who suffer from chronic non-tubercular lung disease should avoid competition in favor of mild, fairly short endurance runs, preferably with other runners. They should not run in places where the breathing passages could become irritated, such as busy streets, areas with high pollen counts, and dusty athletic fields. They should also avoid training in cold, damp, or very hot weather. Asthma sufferers generally have more difficulty in the morning than in the afternoon or evening.

With chronic liver diseases such as fatty liver, chronic liver inflammation/hepatitis, and cirrhosis of the liver, increased levels of liver enzymes can be avoided through more efficient use of energy in performing muscle work. However, an acute or increased bout of hepatitis is cause for ceasing all physical activity. In the case of blood vessel disease such as varicose veins and post-thrombotic syndrome, gentle running on a springy surface can help; swimming is even better. Weight lifting, rowing, and cycling are not recommended. Chronic dialysis patients (with artificial kidneys) can benefit from training. It improves their ability to perform since oxygen is transported more quickly to the tissues and is utilized more effectively once it gets there.

Endurance training also has a positive effect on the risk factors already mentioned in the context of heart and circulatory diseases such as gout (elevated levels of uric acid in the blood), mild forms of high blood pressure (arterial hypertonia), elevated blood lipid levels, and obesity (adiposity). With all the diseases mentioned, *medical supervision of training supported by regular testing is absolutely essential* in order to avoid dangers and to determine an appropriate amount of training.

Health Risks Associated with Running

Heat Injuries

Under extreme climatic conditions of heat and high humidity, exceptional physical demands, such as in a marathon, can produce a buildup of heat in the body. The body temperature climbs to a rectal temperature of 108 degrees Fahrenheit (42 degrees Centigrade), the runner experiences emotional changes such as sudden aggressiveness followed by disorientation, blurred consciousness, and finally circulatory collapse. This is known as heatstroke. There is a particular danger with the use of stimulants (amphetamines), which help highly motivated athletes exceed the limits of their vital reserves.

Immediate countermeasures include lying down in a cool, darkened area, careful cooling with cold wraps and rubdowns, and additional infusions of fluids and electrolyte replacements. In contrast with that situation, sunstroke is a direct effect of the sun's rays when they fall on a person's unprotected head; children are particularly susceptible. This results in heat buildup in the head, which feels hot, while the body remains mostly cool. There is an onset of stiffness in the neck and nausea. Here, too, a cool, shady spot is required followed by cold wraps for the head. Heat exhaustion occurs with copious sweating in combination with insufficient fluid intake and is triggered by a volume deficiency. The skin becomes pale since the blood vessels in the skin contract and that, in turn, increases the body temperature. This should be treated with fluids that are not too cold.

If a lot of salts are also lost with sweat and are not replaced by appropriate electrolyte drinks, heat cramps in the muscles may result—especially in the calf muscles. Passive stretching of the muscle can relieve the cramp, but ultimately the needed salt must be supplied.

In order to prevent heat injuries, it is advisable to take at least four days to acclimatize yourself if you want to compete in unaccustomed heat or humidity. Training should take place in carefully controlled amounts and in approximately the same conditions (e.g., location and time of day) as the competition. Altogether, you should be exposed to the sun at least four hours a day. Vitamin C (about 250 milligrams per day), and of course lots of fluids and sufficient electrolytes, will help you get used to the heat.

It is interesting to note that for every 0.04 ounces (1 g) of sweat that evaporates fully, the body gets rid of 586 calories of heat. However, a large amount of sweat usually drips off and is thus lost to the cooling process.

Side Stitches

Regular endurance training over the years leads to enlargement of the

liver, but this is not to be confused with illness. The liver remains fully functional, and the increase in size is merely an adjustment to greater demands. In this regard, top-level athletes practically never experience side stitches under the right costal arch.

The situation is different, though, after a rest period when enlargement in the liver or spleen in the upper left abdomen has decreased. Increased blood flow can lead to stretching of the connective capsule and to side stitches. Often deep, exaggerated breathing or hill running can help relieve the situation.

Fluids—inside and out—protect against overheating.

Heat regulation in the human body as a function of air temperature (based on Lehmann). At temperatures over 95 degrees Fahrenheit (35 degrees Centigrade), the body can eliminate heat only through evaporation of sweat. The effectiveness of this process increases as the external temperature rises. In the absence of adequate fluids, sufficient sweat can no longer be produced. That inevitably leads to overheating in the body.

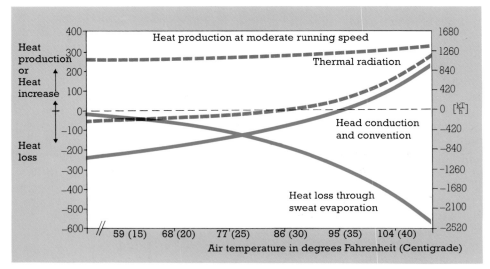

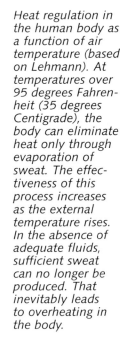

This can also occur if a person trains too soon after a big meal. With the movement of running, the full structures of the digestive tract (stomach and small intestine) pull against their suspension points, and that may likewise produce discomfort in the abdomen.

Digestive Complaints

If training and competition are frequently interrupted by digestive problems, runners should carefully examine their dietary habits.

The body performs the majority of its digestive work about an hour-and-a-half after a meal. During this time it is surely inappropriate to run. It is best to wait two-and-a-half to three hours after the last meal, and that should not be too rich in fiber or cause undue distention.

The fermentation process of carbohydrate digestion appears to be essentially less taxing to the body than the decay process involved in protein digestion. A few days of eating fruit, vegetables, and grain products can therefore help regulate upset digestive processes.

While your body uses carbohydrates to fuel its physical activities, certain types of carbohydrates may actually cause digestive problems and speed gastric emptying—that is, cause diarrhea in runners. If you develop diarrhea or gas during or after your runs, review your diet to see how much fiber and fruit you may be eating prior to your runs. Cutting back on fruit sugars (in whole fruits or drinks) may help. Cutting back on bran may also be necessary. However, all fruits and fibers are not a problem. Including a bit more rice or bananas can, in fact, firm up soft stools. You may need to see a sports-oriented doctor who can suggest medication to help relieve the problem.

Early Summer Meningoencephalitis

In certain areas where diseases are prevalent, there is an increased risk of being bitten by ticks. That allows the ticks to transmit viruses to people and cause meningitis. Runners are particularly at risk since they wear light clothing and train in the woods and parks in the warm weather. The most sensible precautionary measure is a timely inoculation. If you are bitten by a tick and have not already had a shot, you should get one immediately.

Running and Injuries to the Musculoskeletal System

It should be possible for any orthopedic doctor with at least a mild interest in sports to facilitate a runner's entry into the world of training. If there are any unrecognized preexisting conditions, running may aggravate them and lead to more serious illnesses. Preventive measures are often simple, as long as they are begun early enough.

Knee Problems

Even without medical training, most people have a clear idea of what a straight leg should look like. Small amounts of play significantly change the stress relationships in the knee. Bowed legs (genu varum) place more stress onto the inner (medial) part of the knee. On the other hand, knock-knees (genu valgum) place the pressure onto the outside of the knee. There may be additional stress problems in related joints such as the ankle and foot.

As a result of excessive mechanical demands, the knee experiences degenerative changes such as damage to the menisci, stretched tendons, and damaged cartilage, which may lead to arthrosis (stiffening in the joints).

In mild cases, a shoe insert that raises the inside or outside edge may be adequate; in many cases the abnormality will even be tolerated without complaint. Extreme cases require an operation to set the bones straight (corrective osteotomy).

than the related prehensile feet of apes. Next to the spine, they have the most to complain about as a result of walking upright! Fashion is another cause for complaint.

When squeezed into unspeakable shoes, for many hours every day feet have to carry loads that often exceed several times body weight, about two to three times body weight while running. For that purpose, they have developed flexible, elastic arches but have given up such functions as grasping and clutching. Greater stability means less flexibility.

Foot Deformities

The foot is a prime example of the variety that biological systems have evolved to meet different living conditions and demands (horse, deer, ape, frog, bird, etc.). Human feet have developed differently

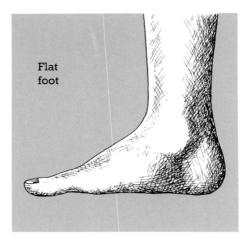

Flat foot

The long arch is completely sunken, and the inside edge of the foot contacts the ground.

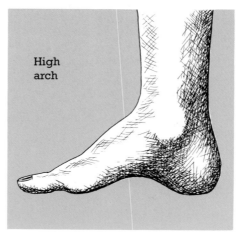

High arch

Exceptionally high arch, the outer edge of the foot does not make continual contact with the ground.

Normal height of arch, the outer edge of the foot is in consistent contact with the ground.

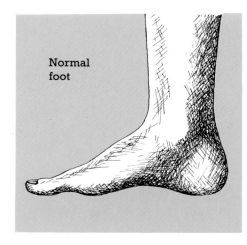

Normal foot

The long arch is like a right triangle whose shorter side is formed by the heel bone and the longer side by the ankle and midfoot.

The flat tendons in the sole of the foot (plantar aponeuroses), plus the tendons and muscles in the sole and calf that move the toes, make it possible to place this flexible yet sturdy construction under tension for many years. Only living structures with their limitless powers of regeneration could tolerate such countless changes in load for a long period of time.

A special stirrup function is assumed by the long calf muscle (peroneus longus) and the rear shin muscle (tibialis posterior). In the forefoot, the diagonal arch spans between the first joints of the big and little toes. It relieves the stress on the tendons of the muscles that move the toes and the ankles between the bones of the midfoot and the main parts of the toes. Changes in the arch always produce increased stress on the affected structures. It is especially necessary to protect the joints since it is hard for sensitive cartilage to repair itself once it is injured. Even tendons react sensitively to overload.

The foot demonstrates its capabilities in motion, especially when running. Healthy, flexible feet of children exhibit a movement known as *torsion*; it has influenced the construction of athletic shoes. If the front of your foot moves in the valgus direction when you stand on tiptoes (that is, if the outer edge of the foot or the outer toes lift up), the back of the foot describes the opposite movement: the heel turns in the varus direction, whereby the heel bone rotates inward. This stabilizes the foot, which in a complete tiptoe stance rests on only the first axis (or a straight line projected along the big toe).

Exterior side view of human foot.

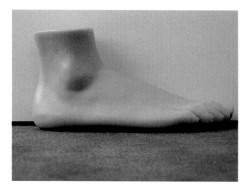

Interior side view of human foot showing arch (left).

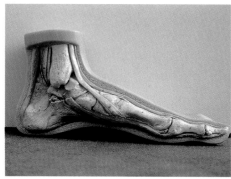

X ray of human foot in running motion (right).

A foot that lacks muscular support collapses under the pressure of the body weight and the continued load bearing involved in walking, standing, and running. The flattening of the long arch produces fallen arches and, in extreme cases, flat feet. At the same time, the heel bone turns inward, tipping the foot. Often the cause is weakness in the connecting tissue. Also, the wrong type of footwear can lead to flattening of the arch; this often involves excessively short shoes that are worn during childhood.

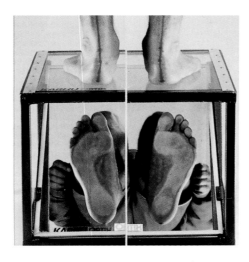

The podoscope permits visual examination of foot dynamics. Here we see feet that are tipped and splayed and that have sunken arches.

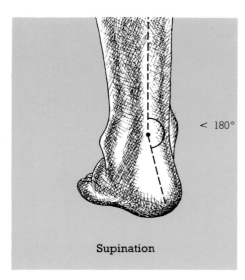

Supination

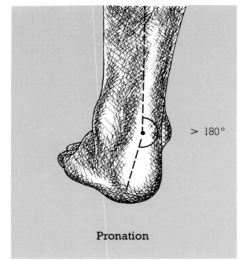

Pronation

Supination (left): Tipping of the heel bone outward (as with typical distortion trauma in the ankle). The angle $\alpha < 180°$.

Pronation (right): The heel bone tips inward (e.g., while running). The angle $\alpha > 180°$.

With splayed feet, the causes are similar; they are produced by excessively short, narrow shoes and heels that are too high. The diagonal arch of the forefoot sinks. As a result, the main load from the first and fifth midfoot bones is transferred to the second through fourth toes. This produces pain in their main joints, a broadening of the forefoot, and, because of the altered orientation of the pulling muscles to hallux valgus, a turning of the big toe outward in the direction of the little toe. Shortening in the muscles that bend the toes leads to hammertoes and clawtoes.

Splayed feet can be corrected with shoe inserts of appropriate size

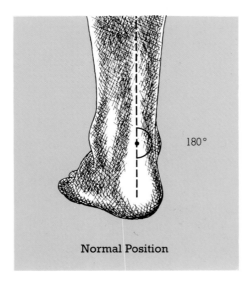

Normal Position

Normal position: The axes of the heel bone and the lower leg coincide. The angle $\alpha = 180°$.

Left: Appearance of hallux valgus.

Right: Orthopedic shoe inserts for runners should be made of synthetic materials and be full length.

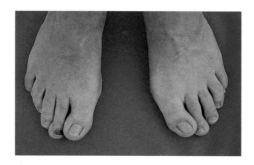

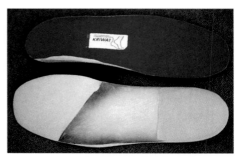

that are usually worn inside the running shoes and the street shoes. Passive correction of improper foot alignment can be complemented by cushioning pressure points, taping the foot, providing an insert for the toes, and other applications—but only as long as they are worn. If the hallux valgus is fully developed, sometimes the only remedy is an operation. This usually produces good results, such as freedom from discomfort, however at the expense of being able to push off with the big toe.

As a result of splayed feet, runners sometimes complain of pains in the middle of the foot. These are caused by the thickening of a nerve ending (known as Morton's neuralgia). Inserts for splayed feet (orthotics) can bring relief; otherwise, it is advisable to separate the lumps surgically.

High arches are another type of physical variation that frequently leads to complaints. The arch is excessively high, often in combination with a heel bone that tips inward. One cause of high arches is an inherently excessive muscle tone that causes the formation of taut, inflexible connecting tissue. Usually, shortening of various muscle groups can be detected. Foot exercises should be used in an attempt to restore flexibility to the foot.

In any case, for healthy feet that will bear the load, runners need properly fitting shoes that are long enough and of the proper width as well as functioning foot muscles. Regular foot exercises can increase the mobility and the strength of the feet. The following exercise program done once or twice every week serves a protective function and checks the progress of any preexisting problems.

Side view and podoscopic picture of feet with high arches.

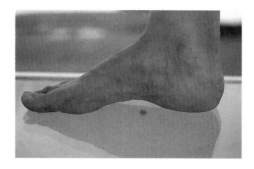

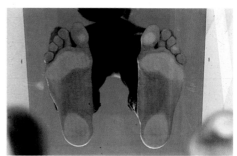

Exercises for Strengthening the Foot Muscles

① Corn Box

A big wooden box or a bucket is filled with dried corn kernels. As you walk in it barefoot, lift the unweighted knee up to horizontal. Stabilize for a moment on the support leg, and then change. Of course, this also works on any type of natural surface (lawn, sand, stony beach or streambed, etc.). Walking or running barefoot is an excellent type of training, but it should be used in carefully measured doses. Most feet are no longer used to good things.

You can also dig down deep with your feet in a bucket. Powerful movements (raising and lowering the front of the feet and the toes or lifting the inner and outer edges of the feet) strengthen the foot muscles all around.

the floor and draw it toward you. As an alternative, you can pick up a pencil using your toes.

③ Foot Top

This strengthens the foot and especially the calf muscles. Stand on the top using one leg. Keep the support leg slightly bent. The free

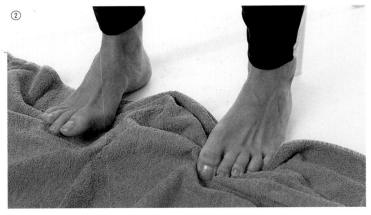

② Grasping Exercises

This serves to strengthen the muscles that bend the toes, the plantar aponeurosis, and the arch. While seated, grasp a towel spread out on

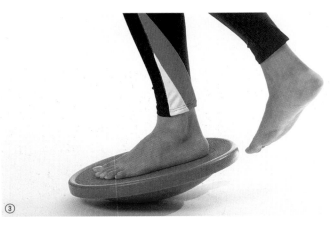

③

③

leg is slowly held out as far as possible to the side and then crossed over the support leg (repeat eight times).

While standing on the foot top, catch a ball that a helper tosses (bad throws make this harder to do!).

④ **Foot Boards**
First a little handiwork is called for. Nail a piece of wood with a rounded cross section to each of four small boards about the size of your foot; nail one lengthwise, one straight across, and two on the diagonal. Try to balance on them using just one foot in such a way that the board

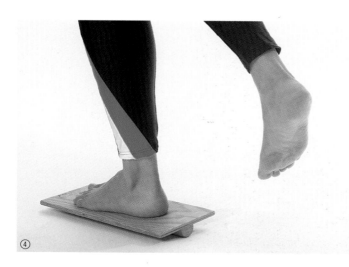

④

④

does not touch the floor. Distractions (see the "Foot Top") are welcome.

⑤ Jumping Exercises

Jumping rope (one leg, two legs, striding in place) strengthens the entire network of straightening muscles in the legs. It is also an effective type of endurance training, and many athletes use it daily.

⑤

⑥ Stretching

Stretching exercises round the program out. They are especially good for the calf muscles (the gastrocnemius, stretching the back of the leg—and bending the long peroneus muscle) and the shin muscles (sitting on the heels in a kneeling position).

⑥

⑥

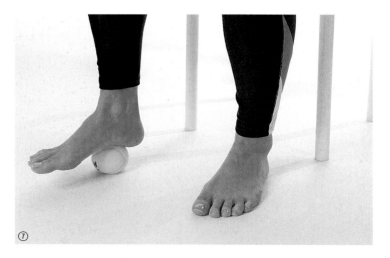

⑦ Promoting Circulation

In a sitting position, roll a tennis ball or other type of ball back and forth under the sole of your foot. The massage effect promotes circulation and simultaneously provides some gentle stretching of the small muscles in the foot.

⑧ The dermapuncture massage has been a respected treatment for quite a while. It can be used successfully not only on the feet and lower legs but also for prevention and treatment of many types of strains. As you massage using the small wheels fitted with silver-plated points, you improve circulation, relax the muscles, and relieve pain.

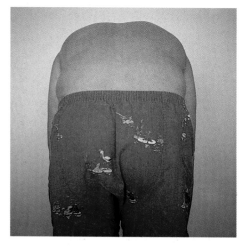

Asymmetry in the rib cage (which is most visible with the body leaning forward) may be a sign of a difference in leg length.

Unequal Leg Length

Among humans, legs of equal length are an exception. There is usually a difference amounting to a couple of millimeters. A more pronounced difference in leg length, however, may cause the pelvis to tip to one side and the spine to compensate with a bend (known as compensatory scoliosis). This leads to asymmetry in the rib cage, which can often be seen clearly with the upper body leaning forward. The exact measurement of the difference in leg length can be determined only with X rays—a standing pelvic panorama.

In order to prevent complaints in the spine, the sacroiliac or iliosacral joint, or the spinal erectors, a length difference of 0.39 to 0.59 inches (1.0 to 1.5 cm) should be corrected. The longer it has existed, the more care is required, and only a partial correction is appropriate. Ideally, one shoe should have a full-length lifter in the midsole area. This is also the best arrangement for use with other

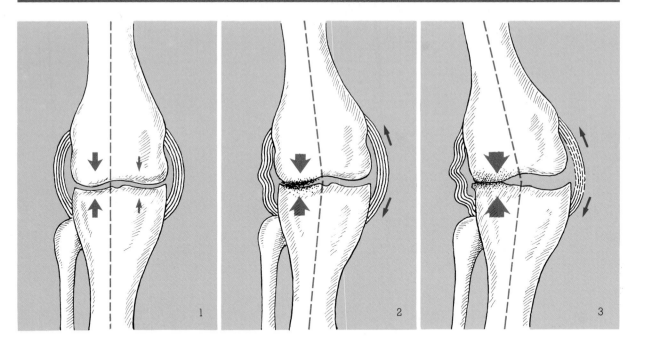

measures such as wraps, wedges, and so forth. With small differences in leg length, shoe inserts can be used even though they make the shoe tighter and may slip.

Prearthrosis and Arthrosis

Arthrosis involves the closing up of a joint; prearthrosis refers to the types of disease that lead to that condition. The most important structure for the function of a joint is cartilage. In combination with synovial fluid (a type of lubricant), it permits nearly friction-free gliding and rolling of the joint surfaces against one another. Cartilage is very resistant to pressure, but it can be damaged by sudden, simultaneous lateral forces (shear stress), which joints are not equipped by nature to handle. The most common example is arthrosis of the joint between the kneecap (patella) and the thigh bone (femur), or femoropatellarthrosis. As an example, the extremely high stresses placed on the knee in doing deep squats with weights, combined with faulty tech-

nique, can lead to tremendously high pressure (over 4,400 pounds/2,000 kg per 0.061 cubic inches/1 square cm), tear the synovial lubricating film, and destroy the cartilage. Other causes are joint instability that may result from loose connective tissue (congenital or resulting from an accident) or improper relationships between joint surfaces.

At first, the joint becomes weak. Later, the meniscus and cartilage may separate. If a cure is effected, it involves formation of scar tissue with inferior cartilage fibers since the body cannot build any new cartilage cells. As excessive and improper stress accumulates, cartilage defects arise that expose the bones. Significant pain, functional loss, and loss of mobility then characterize the complete onset of arthrosis.

Improper alignment can be corrected surgically in order to improve the functioning of the joint (if stretching and strengthening exercises do not work). The goal is to optimize the coordination or the unimpaired interplay of all structures in the movement apparatus.

Improper alignment in the knees: (knock-knees) with development of what is known as valgus gonarthritis.

155

Early treatment consists of eliminating the harmful causes to the extent possible. Improper alignments must be corrected (perhaps surgically), and the functioning of the muscles and tendons has to be optimized. The choice of sports must be subordinated to health concerns. Regular running does not lead to arthrosis in the presence of healthy, properly aligned limbs and adequate running technique, even after many years. On the other hand, some sports foster onset and development of joint injuries with great stress peaks (weight lifting and triple jump, for example) or frequent tiny injuries (such as soccer and handball). In the presence of arthrotic changes, sports including running should not be done strenuously. However, light athletic activity, muscle strengthening, and specific exercises can be used as functional movement therapy. They help promote metabolism in the joint, maintain the range of movement, and thereby prevent permanent muscle shortening.

Swimming, cross-country skiing, bicycling, and especially aqua jogging in mild forms are very beneficial.

Flattened Back, Rounded Shoulders, and Arched Back

Most misalignments in the spine are the result of muscle weakness and imbalances. As long as they are correctable (that is, responsive to balancing through active use of the muscles of the torso), they are not considered a disease in the proper sense of the word. The use of a strong muscle corset can also help correct many cases of improper vertebral alignment. However, when improper alignment persists for a long time, it can lead to serious changes in the spine. So if back pain occurs early in life (usually during puberty), a doctor should be consulted so that serious disorders of the growing spine can be eliminated.

In order to improve or entirely eliminate improper alignment. It is a good idea to strengthen the appropriate muscles. Running should be complemented with mobility

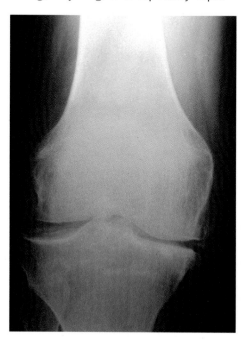

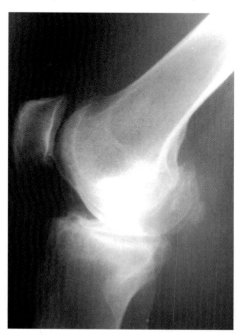

Left:
X ray of varus gonarthritis. The shrinking of the inner knee fissure is evident as well as the thickening of the bone near the fissure and the incipient bony lip that signifies excess stress on the joint resulting from bowed legs.

Right:
Arthrosis between the rear surface of the kneecap and the contact area with the thigh bone (femoro-patelarthrosis).

exercises and strength training for back and stomach muscles.

Runners are a special type of people since they swim (or run) against the current. The current is the overwhelming majority of our compatriots who think that physical activity is something that needs to be banished from daily and professional life. Elevators and escalators, remote controls, and robots were not invented by runners.

Runners also do not suffer from the problems that today's average civilized person must cope with. They do not suffer from being overweight, shortness of breath when they climb stairs, or worries about cholesterol levels. Yet, running seems to fail in one very important area. Back pain is the number-one reason people take sick days from work,

and runners are not exempted from that.

On closer observation, that is not too surprising since running as an endurance sport affects primarily the organs and the musculoskeletal system to a much lesser degree. The latter must at least work properly, contribute to the effort, and pose as few additional demands as possible! Many runners have had the painful experience of dealing with the quick onset of unexpected problems.

Running is a natural, primeval type of exercise that in no way endangers the spine. On the contrary, the continuous shift between stress and relaxation is considered to be beneficial for nourishing the connective tissue, as long as the vertebrae are aligned properly and the genetically prescribed basic double

Aqua jogging is one of the most effective and gentle complementary sports for runners.

157

S-shaped curve is safeguarded. For that purpose, runners need several skills that are not directly related to their qualities as endurance athletes:

1. **Coordination** (movement and running style that are appropriate for the back);
2. **Strength** (in the muscles of the torso and the contiguous extremities); and
3. **Flexibility** (in the spine itself and the surrounding structures, especially the muscles).

Coordination

The same ground rules as for daily life apply to a running style that safeguards the spine. An upright position should be maintained as much as possible in order to avoid shocks, bends, and twists.

That is made possible by planting the foot at the level of the joint of the small toe and cushioning every step with the joints and muscles. That becomes more difficult when the foot is planted heel first; plus the front of the foot is lifted higher than the heel. That can lead to short-term and possibly violent overextending in the lumbar vertebrae—a movement that is similar to the technique that people formerly used in the long jump.

The head should be held erect. That also keeps the rib cage up, and breathing is freer. That also avoids a common posture defect: we are almost always compelled to work, eat, and read with our upper body leaning forward to a greater or lesser degree. As a result, the back becomes rounded in the area of the thoracic vertebrae, the ventral chest muscles shorten, and the dorsal muscles (on and between the shoulder blades) atrophy. This is a vicious circle with fatal consequences (posture problems, impairment of the breathing process, and decreased performance), which are often observed in older people. So avoid rounded shoulders by running! It is better to run through the neighborhood with your head in the air than with a humble, lowered gaze, and not just from an orthopedic viewpoint.

Strength

A modicum of strength is a prerequisite for erect posture. The spinal column is like a staff composed of 25 movable parts. In addition to the various ligaments (sinewy structures with a certain elasticity), it is stabilized by a real network of muscular cords. Their proper functioning depends on regular use. Frequent relaxation (sitting!) leads to loss of strength or atrophy. The essential corset effect of the upper body muscles diminishes. That increases the strain on the ligaments and joints in the spine, especially the pressure on the disks—the first step in developing back pain. Muscles in particular danger of weakening include the rectus abdominis, the gluteus medius, and the rhomboid muscles.

When you run, you subject your body to high stress, about two to three times body weight with every step. This must be stabilized in space, on uneven surfaces, on hills, and over long distances. If the muscles in the torso, pelvis, and hips are overburdened, improper stresses arise and coordination suffers (see above). Running is endurance training. So strength needs to be developed separately. The load in strength training for upper body muscles should permit a maximum of 25 to 40 repetitions per exercise (strength endurance training). Usually your own body weight is adequate for that (especially if it is a little too high!). If weights are to be used, it is particularly important to do the exercises technically cleanly (with good coordination).

You can get a fairly reliable idea of how strong your upper body muscles are by doing a couple of simple tests. If you can maintain the given position for a specified amount of time, your upper body muscles are in good shape. However, if they start to tremble before then, some strengthening exercises are called for.

Agility

Shortened muscles are usual in people who are not in shape, and they are not even too uncommon among athletes. In some sports, they are the rule. Runners usually do stretching exercises regularly and conscientiously, and for good reason. Take, for instance, the pelvis. When seen from the side, it can be compared to a turntable in the middle of the body. If any of the muscle groups that involve the pelvis become shortened, they can affect its position. The pelvis may tip too far forward or to the rear, and that, in turn, has implications for the lumbar vertebrae. Then it is the same old story: a change in the position of the spine, imperfect coordination, strain, and pain.

For every type of back exercise there is a corresponding stretching exercise. These are important for the muscles that tend to shorten include the iliopsoas, the straight thigh muscle (rectus femoris), and the spinal erectors.

Exercises for the spine should not be regarded as a tedious matter for mature people. Well-trained runners should not feel that these are just silly exercises that can be done blindfolded or piecemeal. A conscientious program of back exercises can produce improved motor skills. It may also help you put one over on the statistic that says that back pain is the principle cause of lost time from work.

Diagnostic Exercises (Illustration on p. 160)

The following three exercises should enable you to test the fitness of your upper body muscles. These tests are merely a point of reference and are not conclusive evidence of possible deficits in strength or flexibility.

① Frontal Elbow Support Using Both Legs

Place your forearms onto the floor parallel and shoulder-width apart; keep upper arms vertical. Feet are about hip breadth apart. Lift up your body, and hold it completely straight. Your bottom should not be raised too far, and your belly should not sag down. Tell yourself, "Steady, now!" Hold your head straight as an extension of your body. You should hold this position without trembling.

30 seconds—good

20 seconds—improvement needed

10 seconds—not strong enough for running

② Rear Support Using One Leg

Place your hands behind your body about shoulder width apart, fingertips point downward and outward. Feet are placed hip width apart on the heels. Point your toes upward and straighten your knees.

Lift your body up from the floor so that it is completely straightened. Keep the muscles of the buttocks, stomach, and lower back taut. At that point, keep one leg straight and lift it up about the length of one foot without twisting your pelvis or dropping your bottom. Stop when your body begins to tremble.

20 seconds—very good

10 seconds—improvement needed

0 seconds— not strong enough (position cannot be stabilized)

159

③ Hamstring Stretches

Lie flat on your back. Lift up one leg so that the thigh is vertical. Hip is at a right angle. Grab your upper leg with your hands to provide some resistance, and then slowly straighten your knee.

0° = complete straightening of knee— good flexibility

15° short of full straightening— improvement needed

30° short of full straightening— heightened risk of back injury

Strengthening Exercises

The upper body muscles work statically to stabilize the spine through long hours every day. Exercises should be done slowly. As you tense the muscles, you should breathe out forcefully. Let the air flow passively back into your lungs during the relaxation stage. Forced breathing that raises your blood pressure should be avoided.

Amount:

Set a goal of three sets of 15 repetitions (for each side); each cycle of lifting, holding, and setting down should last about seven seconds. Two or three times a week is enough for the strengthening exercises. Daily strength training affords no advantages and taxes the muscles' ability to recover.

④ Strengthening the Abdominals

Lie on your back, and bend your knees approximately at right angles. Place your feet onto the floor, and point your toes up forcefully. Tense your stomach muscles, and press your lumbar vertebrae against the floor.

Lift both arms with the palms facing up. Then begin to raise your torso until the shoulder blades are totally off the floor.

Keep the head aligned with the body, and look straight up. Be sure not to jerk your head, force it onto your chest, or use your hands.

⑤ Strengthening Exercises for the Hamstrings, Gluteals, and Spinal Erectors

Lie on your back, and bend one knee at approximately a right angle. Keep your heel on the floor, and lift the toes. Without using your arms, lift your bottom until the upper body is in a completely straight line from the shoulder to the knee. Keep the other leg straight, and hold it up so that both thighs are parallel. Point this foot upward too. In this position, avoid twisting the pelvis toward the raised leg.

The arms are held outward next to the body or parallel to it. Fingertips point outward, and the elbows are slightly bent, as if you wanted to push away an invisible wall.

⑥ Side Support

As you lie on your side, you support your upper body on your forearm placed flat onto the floor. The upper arm is held vertical immediately under the shoulder. Lift up your pelvis, and stabilize your whole upper body so that it forms a straight line. The muscles of the stomach, back, and bottom are tensed. The feet are placed one on top of the other with the toes pulled up. The free hand is placed onto the thigh, and the head is held straight as an extension of the body.

Sometimes exercises are needed to stabilize the body in a side support since this also requires balance. At the beginning, it may help to use the free hand for support.

④

⑤

⑥

Keep your upper body from sinking between the support arms.

The head is held straight as an extension of the body.

⑧ Kneeling Inclines

This exercise is an effective means of counterbalancing the upper body strains we encounter in our everyday and professional lives.

We continually live and work with our upper body tipped forward. Our back is rounded when we eat, read, work at a desk, and do housework. As a result, the strain on the spine is often greater when we are seated than when standing.

As a result of this ongoing, one-sided pressure on the spine, the chest muscles (pectoralis major and minor) become shortened. At the same time, the muscles between the shoulder blades become weaker. As a result, improper posture is reinforced until sooner or later it can no longer be corrected.

Possible consequences include functional deterioration in the lungs and chest organs and persistent pains in the head and neck.

Start by holding your back in a normal position as you kneel on the floor—that is, use your upper body muscles to maintain the slight hollow in your lumbar vertebrae. Hold your arms out to the side at shoulder level with the forearms high in the air. Incline the upper body gently and slowly to the front without reducing the tension in the spinal erector muscles. That way the hollow in the back is maintained.

Simultaneously, the upper arms are brought toward the rear so that the shoulder blades slightly touch one another. Keep the head up, as well as the chest, whose position is supported by deep breathing.

This involves symmetrical stretching of the chest muscles at the same time the shoulder blade muscles are strengthened.

⑦ Frontal Support Using One Leg

Place both forearms onto the floor parallel and shoulder width apart; keep the upper arms vertical. Feet are placed about hip width apart with only the toes touching the floor.

Slowly lift up the body until it forms as straight a line as possible. Tense your stomach, back, and bottom muscles as well as the thighs, and straighten the knees. Lift up one leg about one foot's length from the floor without changing the position of your upper body or pelvis.

With this exercise, it is particularly important to keep the muscles between the shoulder blades taut so that the normal slight curvature of the thoracic vertebrae is preserved.

Stretching Exercises

Stretching exercises are usually used selectively on individual muscles or muscle groups. With no pretension to completeness, here are a few selected stretching exercises.

Stretching exercises can (or perhaps should) be done daily, depending on how tight the particular muscles are. Individual muscle groups can become tight to differing degrees, so some stretching exercises may become more important than others.

Do the stretching exercises slowly and continuously. Above all, avoid violent or bouncing movements that activate the muscles' stretching reflex and reduce the effectiveness of the stretching. Stretching exercises should not be painful. Effective stretching is indicated by a noticeable tenseness in the particular muscle.

You should keep your breathing calm and relaxed as you do the stretching exercises. Be sure not to force your breathing. It is important to support each exercise actively by tensing the opposing muscle group (for example, see the stretching exercises on pages 80 and 85). Each exercise should be held for about 20 to 30 seconds.

⑨ Seated Twists

This exercise stretches the muscles of the bottom and the lower back. For simplicity, this exercise will be described in terms of stretching the gluteals on the right side. For the left side, simply reverse the procedure. Sit on the floor with your knees straight. Lift your right leg, and place your foot to the outside of your left knee. Turn your upper body as far as possible to the right so you can use your left elbow to force your right knee toward the left. Place your right hand far to the rear of your body, and turn your head to the right.

⑩ Hip Stretches for the Iliopsoas

In a lunging stance, bend your forward knee and rest the trailing knee on the floor. Lower the pelvis until you feel tension in the groin area near the rear leg. Tense the gluteals, and use the free hand to push the pelvis ahead gently. The upper body is inclined slightly to the front to form a straight line with the rear thigh (in other words, do not arch the back too much!).

Be sure to place the forward leg far to the front to keep the knee from being bent at greater than a right angle. Otherwise, you will place too much strain onto the knee.

You can use your unemployed hand to reach to the side and support yourself against a wall, railing, or something similar to stabilize your position.

⑪ Bundle

In a knee stand, place your bottom onto your heels and bend your upper body forward until your head touches the floor. Try to make your back as round as possible. The arms lie relaxed next to your body. Breathe out forcefully, and let the air flow in passively.

⑫ Flat on Your Back

Lie flat on your back, and support your lower back with a roll (a towel or small pillow, for example). This will support the natural curvature known as lordosis.

Spread the legs a little. The arms are likewise spread overhead.

In this position, you will feel a certain amount of tension in your stomach muscles.

Stretching and strengthening should complement each other as much as possible. After strengthening exercises, stretching helps reduce the increased muscle tension (e.g., after strengthening the stomach muscles with exercise 4).

⑬ Side Stretches

In a straddle stance with the feet rotated slightly outward, the upper body is slowly bent toward the side without twisting. Chest and face remain in the same plane as the pelvis. One hand rests on the hip, and the other reaches nearly straight overhead, thereby stretching the broad muscle of the back (latissimus dorsi).

⑭ Pect Stretches
(One Side at a Time)

With one foot placed slightly forward, the upper arm of the same side (!) is held out horizontal while the forearm points upward; place the forearm against some resistance (a partner, wall, or tree, for example). Pull the other shoulder rearward so that the body and head are turned away from the raised arm.

This provides passive stretching of the chest muscles (pectoralis majoris).

Osteoporosis

People are inclined to consider bones to be rock hard. It is not well-known that bones are among the most active tissues in the human body and subject to rapid alteration. With as little as one week of confinement to bed (e.g., with the common flu), a healthy person loses 1 to 2 percent of overall bone mass!

Osteoporosis is the commonest bone disease that affects the skeletal system. It comes about through what is referred to as a negative bone balance. Over a fairly long time, more bone material is broken down than is rebuilt. The bone mass decreases, the microarchitecture or framework of the bone is destroyed, and the risk of bone fracture increases.

This is a normal development from age 40 on. About 0.5 to 1 percent of the bone material is lost every year. With the full onset of the illness, up to 6 percent is lost! However, osteoporosis does not affect only elderly women as is commonly believed. One out of three women over the age of 50 suffers a spiral fracture, but even young men and athletes can be affected by a loss of minerals in the bones.

The causes are complex since bone metabolism is controlled by several hormone systems. A greater risk is associated with:
- women as opposed to men;
- thin rather than fat people;
- old rather than young people;
- smokers as opposed to non-smokers;
- alcoholics as opposed to non-drinkers;
- whites as opposed to blacks;
- sedentary workers as opposed to physically active ones; and
- relatives of people who suffer from osteoporosis.

Dietary habits also play an important role. Calcium is the most common mineral in the human body. Vitamin D makes it possible to absorb calcium from food, use it for building bones, and encourage bone growth. Lack of calcium (in milk products, eggs, green cabbage, and broccoli) or vitamin D (in fish, eggs, and liver) are the most common nutritional factors in the onset of osteoporosis.

The male and female sex hormones are particularly important. Both testosterone and estrogen have a protective effect—as does regular athletic activity. If women train too intensively, there is a danger of amenorrhea, a suppression of the regular monthly period. Even with completely "normal" training, there can be some disturbances in complex hormone regulation.

In a 1994 study conducted in Capetown, South Africa, it was possible to attribute occurrences of osteoporosis in young female runners to irregular or suppressed menses. Obviously, training is not the only reason; there are others, such as dietary habits and even psychological factors. It seems that the risk of menstrual disturbances (and attendant mineral disorders in the bones) is higher if the daily caloric intake is inadequate (i.e., in cases of anorexia). Poor eaters, especially girls, may be at risk for osteoporosis!

Menstrual irregularities therefore have far-reaching effects and should not be underestimated. They are an early warning system for bone metabolism and should always be treated by a doctor.

However, bone can regenerate to a certain degree if the hormones return to normal. However, even after regular menstruation resumed, the bone mass in the South-African runners in the study remained reduced in comparison with others whose menses had not been interrupted.

There is a logical connection among hormone disorders, bone density, and the risk of stress fracture (hairline crack in bone). A mineral-depleted bone is less resistant to continually changing stresses of weight and bending, as with each step and every jump. An inorganic substance such as metal or plastic could withstand the stresses that come to play on the lower extremities only for a short while and certainly not for a person's life. The only thing that makes it possible for bones to continue functioning for many decades is the continuous construction and regeneration of bone structure. If this reconstruction is disturbed (e.g., by a lack of building materials), the bone will break apart, either suddenly in response to a blow or eventually in the case of a stress fracture.

How can you tell if you have osteoporosis or are in danger of contracting it? The short answer is that at first you do not notice anything different about the bones! At the outset, osteoporosis is not painful. Only preventive checkups can provide the information, and even they are not 100 percent reliable. Currently, the preferred processes use DEXA scan to measure bone density. Many runners do not know their bones are getting weaker until they develop a series of stress-related injuries, such as stress fractures or shin splints. A prudent doctor can see this history (may notice that the female runner is not having regular menstrual periods) and suggest a DEXA scan to determine bone density. Once the problem has been diagnosed, a small change in diet can help get the body back onto track. There are some medications that show promise in treating osteoporosis, but the best treatment is still prevention.

The best policy is to reduce the risk as much as possible. This includes a well-balanced diet with sufficient calories, calcium, and vitamin D, sensible training (regular running helps, but excessive strain endangers the bones), and watching for early warning signals (e.g., menstrual disorders and loss of appetite).

Disk Injuries

The causes of disk injuries are primarily degenerative in nature. They are the price that we have to pay for walking upright and for a civilized lifestyle. Constitutional factors, improper posture, inadequate muscle tone, and professional strains (sitting!) hasten the process of wear and may lead to disk problems such as prolapse and herniated disk. The gelatinous content of the intervertebral disks is forced outward through a separation in the surrounding connective tissue. It interferes with movement and can press on the neighboring nerve, causing pain down one leg (sciatica) and sensory disorders including numbness and even paralysis.

A few simple but effective measures can be used both preventively and after conservative treatment (primarily rest, pain management, and reducing inflammation) or surgical removal should take place to be sure that the condition does not recur. The most important measures are proper posture and muscle training. When you sit, bend over, and lift weights, the spine should be kept as straight and erect as possible (by bending the knees!). The strain is greatest when you round your back and lift heavy objects. A flat surface that is not too hard is best for sleeping.

In conjunction with the foregoing, the upper body muscles should be strengthened conscientiously (see exercises on page 160). Physical therapy measures can also help, such as topical application of heat, massages, baths, swimming using the crawl and backstrokes, and aqua jogging in warm water. Regular running can be done even after suffering a disk injury—assuming a gentle running style, proper upper-body stability, and of course absence of pain.

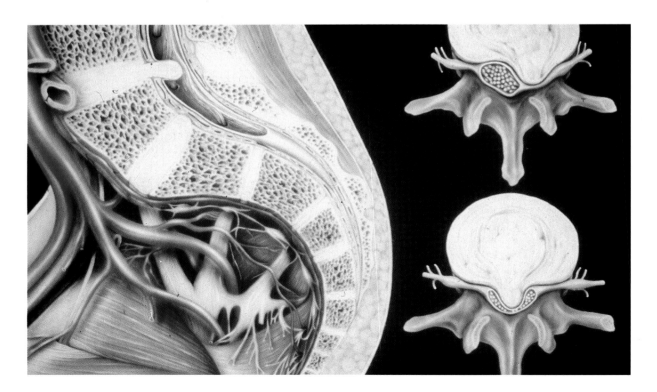

Acute Injuries to the Musculoskeletal System Caused by Running

Muscle Cramps

Muscle cramps are due to the straining of particular muscle groups and are caused by lack of electrolytes, fluids, or oxygen or by some other hypersensitivity. Good conditioning and early electrolyte replacement, especially of magnesium and calcium, can help prevent cramps. Treatment of an acute case consists of stretching the affected muscle group until the cramp subsides and replacing fluids and electrolytes. Massage and rubbing with ice packs may also help.

Blisters

These result from shear stresses or tangential forces between different layers of skin, where tissue fluids, and even blood in the case of

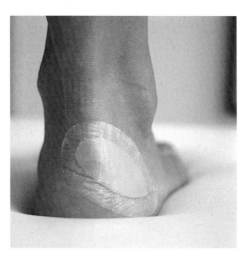

damage to blood vessels, can accumulate. You can prevent blisters by wearing dry, acrylic socks. However, if you get them, you can treat small blisters yourself. Lance the blister with a disinfected needle to let the fluid out. Then the skin must be carefully disinfected and covered with a sterile wrap such as a Second Skin. You can also use a firm foam rubber patch that surrounds the blister without touching it. Occasionally, the treatment has to be repeated. At first, the outer layers of skin should be left in place since they provide protection for the new skin that forms underneath.

Larger, painful, or red and inflamed blisters should be treated by a doctor.

Blackened Toenails

After careful cleansing and disinfecting, the nail is drilled through in one or more places to let the blood out; this is best done by a doctor. Then the site is again disinfected and covered with a sterile dressing. The nail should be left in place. Otherwise, the bed of the nail will become deformed, and the new nail will be crooked and lopsided. Blackened nails are almost an infallible indication that the shoes do not fit right; usually they are too short.

Skin Injuries

With clean surface wounds, disinfection and sterile dressing are all that is needed. In other cases, a doctor should clean and dress the wound. Every athlete should have a current inoculation for tetanus! If you are not up-to-date, you need a combination shot for passive, short-term plus active, long-lasting protection.

Here is the SICK rule for first aid for acute injuries:
S = Stop
I = Ice
C = Compress
K = Keep it elevated

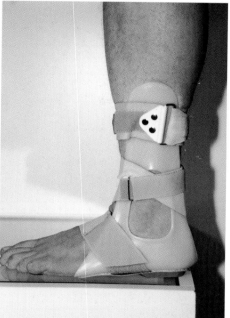

Ankle brace

Bruises (Contusions)

With rough blows, there is always a danger of interior injuries to organs, bones, blood vessels, and nerves, so a thorough check is always advisable. In order to keep bleeding and swelling to a minimum, first aid measures include applications of cold (ice packs, ice water wraps, etc.), compresses, and elevating the affected area.

Cold treatments should be carried out with breaks over the course of several hours. Each treatment should last about eight minutes. Cover the skin with a thin towel to avoid cold injury. An exercise treatment should be begun as soon as possible. This consists of isometric muscle contractions (tensing the muscles without moving the limb) followed by stretching exercises and careful movement in warm water. Heat application and massages are to be avoided.

Sprains

In runners, the most common sprain occurs in the upper part of the ankle—the widely recognized sprained ankle. First aid measures in this case likewise include cold applications, compresses (wraps), elevating the foot, and rest. The extent of the injury and any further therapy required should be determined by careful examination and perhaps an X ray. If one or more ligaments are torn, six weeks of rest in an ankle brace may be required. After surgical repair to ligaments, there is an even chance of recovery as long as the brace is worn consistently (all day and all night). Too often, we see long-term damage ranging from stretched ligaments to arthritis after insufficient treatment of a presumed trifling injury. Throughout the day a stabilizing shoe can also be used. It incorporates supports that restrict lateral movement in the upper ankle while permitting bending and straightening of the foot. On the one hand, that keeps the injured lateral ligaments from strain, and on the other, it avoids trophic disorders such as nutritional deficiencies in the cartilage as a result of long-term immobility. Equally advisable (especially for getting back into training) is a flexible wrap properly applied and changed regularly.

After treatment, intensive movement and strength training are important in restoring complete joint mobility as soon as possible and avoiding subsequent injuries due to strain on other joints, muscles, and tendons.

Joint Dislocations (Luxations)

If the surfaces of a joint are out of normal alignment with one another due to an accident, this is always a serious injury that should be treated only by a doctor—and immediately. In the meantime, keep the joint cool and immobile, and apply measures to counteract the discomfort.

Broken Bones (Fractures)

Pain, bleeding, and improper movement may indicate a fracture. Here, too, the victim must be immediately brought to a doctor. First aid measures include cooling, immobilizing the affected limb with a splint, and pain control. Open fractures where the skin has been broken must be covered with sterile bandages.

Muscle Aches, Knots, Pulls, and Tears

Sore muscles result from intensive, unaccustomed strain and remain painful for a couple of days when the muscles are used or moved. The cause is attributed to eccentric muscle strain that leads to microinjuries to the muscle fibers in the area of the "Z-discs" between the actin-myosin filaments. Eccentric loads are movements in which the muscle is stretched, but its stretching is simultaneously confronted by a resistance, such as in going down stairs or down a hill and the support phase of running on flat terrain. This produces swelling (edema) and pain in the affected muscle fibers.

Cooling with ice and hydropathic treatments, alternating hot and cold baths, mild movement training, and mild stretching may help.

The boundary lines between muscle injuries are imprecise. Muscle knots are the next type of muscle injury. They consist of an altered, long-lasting increase in muscle tension or elevated basic tone. Here, too, simple physical and physiotherapeutic measures such as applications of ice or heat, alternating hot and cold baths, relaxation massages, and stretching exercises may produce the desired results.

If treatment is not successful and the site is injured again, the result can be a vicious circle of pain-functional loss-muscle tightness-pain; it could also result in a pulled muscle. Opinions on the causes of this are divided. People have long suspected excessive stretching or even tearing of individual fibers, but they are also discussing the possibility of an acute compartment syndrome (see page 176) or faulty neuromuscular information transmittal that could result in faulty regulation of muscle tension. When muscle fibers are torn, we are dealing with muscle fibers that are pulled to a greater extent. Treatment consists of careful cooling followed by a wrap that lends compression and support, perhaps even a sling to take the weight off the affected muscle and protect it. Additional aids include foam-rubber wraps, elastic bandages, and non-stretching tape. In the early stages, massages are entirely out of place. When the complaints diminish, active movement exercises should be started as soon as possible. That includes careful, active stretching of the injured muscle, tension exercises with slowly increasing resistance, and then careful movement training (swimming in warm water, bicycling, and aqua jogging, for example). Never go over the pain threshold, and do not place any strain onto the affected muscle until it is absolutely free of pain!

In the case of a torn muscle, which means a tear in a larger, thick part of the muscle, an operation to stitch the muscle back together is usually required—or at least a long, continuous layoff.

Pulled Tendon

Tendon fibers can be injured through uncontrolled, sudden contractions, often in combination with improper stress. This is treated the same way as a pulled muscle, with cold, rest, and a supportive wrap. After an appropriate layoff and disappearance of symptoms, the person can gradually resume training, at first with bicycling and swimming.

Torn Tendon

A torn tendon can be a degenerative injury if it is caused by a sudden muscle tensing (e.g., a torn Achilles tendon while high jumping or playing soccer). Oftentimes, the muscles that are no longer under tension can be observed to bunch up. An operation is needed right away, otherwise the muscle will not be able to take the tension it used to. In the meantime, apply cold and compression, and keep the limb elevated (SICK).

Torn Meniscus

Menisci are somewhat C-shaped, flat structures made of cartilaginous fibers that are not well supplied with blood, and whose exterior wall grows together with the joint capsule. They serve to absorb shocks in the knee and are normally exposed to high pressure through twisting motions and pulling. A healthy meniscus tears only under great stress to the knee, and that can simultaneously produce other injuries such as stretched or torn ligaments and injury to cartilage. A common type of injury in this case is what is referred to as a *basket-handle* tear, where the meniscus is ripped length-

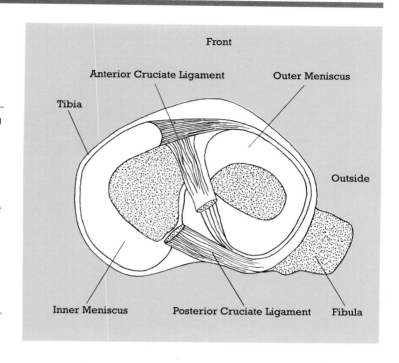

Menisci and cruciate ligaments (top view of shinbone).

wise. When the knee is twisted under load, as in climbing into a car, the tear comes under pressure and causes pain. A doctor can verify this with specific tests during an examination. Nowadays, treatment for a damaged meniscus consists of arthroscopic removal of the torn portion or sewing together the damaged pieces (the all-inside technique). That approach involves penetrating the skin and into the knee capsule in only a couple of spots to do the operation with tiny instruments while observing the process through a lens system hardly as big around as a pencil. The advantage is quick recovery lasting only a few days as opposed to weeks with the common operation where the knee joint is opened up. Joan Benoit Samuelson had arthroscopic knee surgery just 17 days before her 1984 Olympic marathon victory!

Torn Knee Ligaments

Injured knee ligaments, especially the cruciate ligaments, always constitute a threat to knee stability. If given deterioration that ranges from cartilage damage to arthrosis, in most cases an operation is almost unavoidable to restore the strength of this immensely important joint.

With these injuries, too, which often affect several structures in the knee (the so-called unhappy triad of anterior cruciate ligament, inner meniscus, and inner tendon), microinvasive, arthroscopic surgery holds the best promise of success, in part because it greatly improves future prospects for athletic activity. Open knee surgery is considered passé nowadays. With arthroscopy, the torn cruciate ligament is replaced by the body's own tendon tissue either by using a part of the tendon from the kneecap (the patellar tendon) or the tendons of the semitendinous muscle.

Today, people are usually ambulatory during rehabilitation. They may also use therapeutic exercises, muscle-building therapy, and physical therapy. If healing proceeds without complication, easy training may begin four months after an operation. Training that is begun as part of rehabilitation should be continued for several months.

■ Stress Injuries to the Musculoskeletal System Caused by Running

Treatment of stress injuries to the musculoskeletal system still consists in many cases of a pointless series of so-called symptomatic measures (such as radiotherapy, electricity, and injections), including immobilizing a limb in a cast. This type of procedure does not seem to make much sense since it does not deal with the underlying causes. It is more likely that these causes will be aggravated or—in the case of immobilization—complicated by trophic disturbances of muscles and joints. It is almost always better and more effective to use a functional treatment with the goal of restoring the physiological capacities of the affected structures. That includes investigating such things as static stresses (e.g., difference in leg length), muscular imbalances (weakening or shortening of muscles), improper coordination (running style), and training structure.

Inflammation of Gliding Tissue on the Achilles Tendon (Achillodynia)

The Achilles tendon does not really have a sheath, but it is surrounded by a gliding tissue. This normally loose connective tissue contains lots of blood vessels that are needed to supply the tendons, which otherwise are not well supplied with blood. Inflammation does not occur in the tendon itself but rather the gliding tissue, which can harden and in chronic cases, even completely surround the tendon. It reacts degeneratively, as with bloating that weakens it over the long run. Preventive measures, which can be used at the first signs of mild inflammation, include good stretching exercises (see page 81), wearing shoes with a flat heel wedge, hydrotherapy or alternating hot and cold baths for the lower leg, and strengthening exercises for the calf muscles.

To combat an incipient inflammation, you can use ice three times a day for about eight minutes each, especially after training; salves and bandages; ultrasound; and perhaps a temporary heel insert. Treating achillodynia with therapeutic exercises, which is often very effective, involves locally applied diagonal friction and a special technique for massaging tendons. Also, in the early stages, it may be helpful to throw away worn-out running shoes and build some variety into the training program.

Problems with the Achilles tendon often arise after a phase of lengthy endurance training during the winter months that is carried out at a slow pace and perhaps on frozen or softened country paths. With shoes that are too soft and that provide too little stability in the heel, lateral stresses may occur that the tendon cannot tolerate for long periods. Surprising improvements have been obtained in many cases by simply doing incremental runs for 328 to 492 feet (100 to 150 m) on a smooth, solid surface. This involves a clean, coordinated running style at higher muscular tension plus stretching, ice, and perhaps stiffer running shoes.

In the case of advanced, long-standing achillodynia, the only possibilities are treatment by injections (but never directly into the tendon!), radiotherapy, or as a last resort, surgical removal of the scarred, sticky pieces of gliding tissue. Based

on recent experience, immobilizing in a cast, as is still sometimes done, seems to be of no use.

Heel Spurs (Haglund's Exostosis)

The strong pull that the Achilles tendon exerts on the heel bone frequently leads to a thickening of the tarsal knob, which can become severely enlarged. Usually this is caused by an essentially nonpathological predisposition. Inflammation is caused by permanent pressure

Regardless of a person's level of enthusiasm for running, a walking cast is not designed for participating in a citizen's race.

173

from such things as an improperly shaped or excessively hard heel cup in the shoe at first involving the mucous sac (bursa calcanei) and then the surrounding tissue. In addition, achllodynia (see pages 172–173) can also occur where the tendon attaches.

The first step is consistent, conscientious application of stretching exercises to the calf and foot muscles. Additional applications to stem the inflammation include such measures as ice packs and relieving the pressure in the heel area by using a shoe with an open or at least a soft heel.

People who decide to have a heel spur removed or chiseled away surgically face a lengthy convalescence lasting several months or even years.

Irritation of the Outer Knee (Osgood-Schlatter Disease Involving the Tractus Iliotibialis)

Runners sometimes experience irritation on the outer side of the thigh, either 0.8 to 1.6 inches (2 to 4 cm) above the outer knee crease or at the large rolling hill (trochanter major), the bony projection that marks the transition between the pelvic and bottom areas to the thigh region. One cause is overloading the tractus iliotibialis, whose strong tendon glides over the bones at both places and is cushioned by one or several mucous sacs or bursas. This tendon first needs to be stretched by using appropriate exercises. Its hardening is often caused by weakness in the gluteal muscles, so a proper, long-term, and effective cure consists of a strengthening program for this muscle group.

Periostitis (Tendon Inflammation at Insertion Points in the Shin Area)

In most cases, periostitis in runners involves bone sheath inflammation, also commonly known as shin splints. It consists of pain on the inner face of the shinbone around the attachment points of the calf muscles (tendon inflammation of the tibialis posterior). Improper stresses that occur especially when the muscle is stretched while it is tensed or contracted produce irritation at the point where it radiates into the bone. Very pronounced pronation (see pages 20 and 26) or clubfoot and fallen arches can frequently be the cause.

In addition to locally applied measures such as stretching, local diagonal rubbing, and ice, it is important to eliminate the cause of the problem, in this case the over-pronation or any improper stress. This may involve corrections to the running style, foot exercises (see page 151), a change of training shoes, shoe inserts with medial arch supports and heel cup, and other measures.

Groin Pains

Often the tendons of the adductor muscles can become sore at their point of origin at the pubic bone and produce discomfort in the groin. The adductors are the large muscle group on the inside of the thigh that are mostly responsible for bringing the legs together. They also perform other functions such as helping to keep the pelvis stable on the support leg. They are subjected to lots of pressure in such activities as playing soccer and sprinting. The most effective countermeasures include conscientious stretching and local application of ultrasound to stem inflammation. If that does not work, an injection into the painful area may be needed. In chronic cases, surgical notching may be necessary at the point of origin of the muscle. With problems involving the adductors, you should also keep in mind that the strain may be due to weakness in the muscles that are used to stabilize the pelvis (gluteus medius and minimus).

Groin pain can also occur at the pubic bone where the frequently shortened straight stomach muscle (rectus abdominus) radiates or at the origin of the groin ligament. A medical examination can rule out what is known as a *soft groin* or an open groin canal that constitutes a weak point in the abdominal wall.

Kneecap Pain (Patella Point Syndrome)

The kneecap (patella) distributes the pressure that the large thigh muscle (quadriceps femoris) exerts onto the knee joint. Since the kneecap is really built into the tendon in the top part of the kneecap we speak of the quadriceps tendon and of the patellar tendon in the bottom part. The latter originates at the kneecap pole where the patella comes to a point. This leads to certain very high stresses, especially under sudden muscle contraction, such as in jumping and in squatting with free weights. Runners are also occasionally plagued by this type of injury. It is typified by increasing pain as the thigh muscle is tensed against resistance. Preventive measures are comparatively simple: stretching the thigh muscle (quadriceps) and strengthening the muscles on the back of the leg that bend it (hamstring).

Degeneration of the Menisci

The normally high stresses on the menisci may increase further because of faulty bone mechanics such as knock-knees or bowed legs. The increased pressure on one side leads to premature fibrillation or tears (see page 155). A similar effect is produced by instability in the knee due to loosening of the tendons or a genetic weakness in the connecting tissue. Once a meniscus is damaged in its connective structure, there is no cure. In order to protect the joint, especially the cartilage surfaces, from being destroyed by the defective meniscus, at least part of it must be removed. Nowadays, the only sensible way is through arthroscopic means. Healthy meniscus parts must be preserved, even if they are only a tiny strip along the edge. Often, these give rise to regenerated tissue similar in structure to menisci that can take over at least a part of the original function.

Inflammation of the Sole of the Foot (Plantar Aponeurosis)

In conjunction with the muscles in the sole of the foot and other tendons, the plantar aponeurosis spans the arch by stretching from the heel bone to the basal joints of the toes. In the case of flat feet or fallen arches, it comes under greater tension, especially as it radiates into the heel bone. Pain under pressure at the transition from the inner arch to the heel cushion is symptomatic.

Treatment consists of supporting the arch by using inserts and simultaneously removing pressure from the inflamed area by padding it. In addition, the muscles of the foot and toes should be stretched intensively. The cause is almost always a shortening of the muscles that bend the toes. Sometimes local injections are necessary. In chronic cases, a stiff ossification sometimes builds up that is known as a plantar heel spur. Only in exceptional cases should it be removed surgically (with simultaneous periosteal notching).

Compartment Syndrome

Each muscle is embedded in a fascia that surrounds it like a nonstretching sheath. Defects in the fascia produce a protrusion of the muscle, which is referred to as a muscle hernia. The contrary effect occurs when the fascia encloses the muscle so tightly that it interferes with its functioning. A muscle that is working hard is supplied with more blood than a muscle at rest and therefore needs more space. Also, a pathologically elevated muscle tone (muscle hardening or pull) or hemorrhage can temporarily increase the space requirements of a muscle. An excessively tight fascia sheath interferes with blood supply to the muscle and the venous removal of metabolic by-products, and consequently with the muscle's functioning. This most commonly affects the shin, calf, and thigh muscles. Athletes John Walker, Dick Quax, and Mary Decker suffered from a chronically recurring type of this illness.

The problem manifests itself as increasing, strong pains in the affected muscle while running. They subside slowly when the person stops running. In addition, the ability of the muscle to recover is reduced. In serious acute cases, blood supply is so severely restricted that the feet become cold, the skin pale, and the pulse in the feet noticeably weak. Treatment consists of injections to relax the muscles. In emergency cases, surgically notching the fascia always brings results as long as the diagnosis is correct.

Iliotibial Bend Syndrome

The iliopsoas muscle can become hardened and shortened through continuous and improper stress (such as sitting!). This is the strongest muscle in the hip, and it is referred to as *the runner's muscle*. Typically, this condition interferes with complete straightening in the hip joint and produces pain. It can also affect the knee. The stride shortens, and the foot may even turn outward. Treatment consists of regular, consistent stretching exercises, at first preferably with the help of a physiotherapist. Baths and medications can complement that treatment.

Stress Fracture

Sports injuries in the form of stress fractures are on the rise. The causes for this have not yet been fully investigated. Whereas earlier the marching fracture of the second bone in the midfoot of military recruits and the fracture of the navicular bone in the wrist of jackhammer operators were the most common cases, nowadays runners are suffering similar injuries at an increased rate. Most commonly affected are the second midfoot bone, the fibula (usually a hand's breadth above the outer ankle bone), the shinbone, and the navicular bone in the tarsus of the foot.

At first, the microstructure of the bone is destroyed by continuous, harmful bending stresses that exceed the bone's regenerative capacity. Uncharacteristic, incipient pains are experienced, and they do not respond to the usual treatments. If training continues unchanged, the complaints always increase until it becomes practically impossible to continue running.

The first possible diagnostic tool is a bone scan, which indicates accelerated bone renovation in the painful

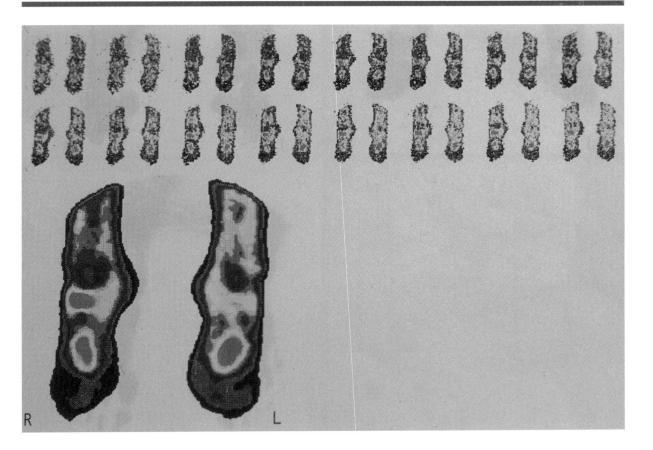

area. This type of investigation has the drawback, though, of being unspecific. Similar findings can be caused by tumors, inflammations, and other problems. In addition, it exposes the patient's body to minor radiation (a radioactive marking substance is injected that accumulates quickly and exclusively in the bones). Only later, usually after some weeks, do the typical changes (such as notching, thickening, and callus formation) become visible on X rays (exploratory X rays and tomograms) or magnetic resonance tomography. Treatment consists especially of keeping close watch on the affected area or even laying off training for a sufficient amount of time. It may be possible to continue aerobic training with bicycling, aqua jogging, and swimming. The important thing is to eliminate the strain that caused the injury for two to three months or even longer, until X rays show that the bone has completely regenerated.

Stress fracture of the navicular bone in the foot (red area) as shown in a bone scintigram with SPECT.

Running Seminars

Ever since 1980, the author of this book has conducted running seminars designed to help a broad range of runners from beginners to advanced. These seminars have nothing in common with some other programs that are designed merely to pile on miles of running. Rather, they are based on the principles set forth in this book to promote successful and injury-free running. Participants decide the amount of running and the goal setting (for purposes of health, recreation, or competition) that are appropriate for themselves. Whatever group they feel they belong in, they are responsible for knowing and mastering the tools of their trade, that is, the basics of training, regulating the workload, the possibilities presented by the exercises that go along with training, and so forth.

A number of distinguished world-class runners help put on these seminars in several European resort areas. All these seminars last for a week and include room, board, and various daily activities.

With the spread of running as a participation sport throughout much of the world, it should be possible to find similar programs offered in many parts of North America. Readers who are interested in spending productive time with likeminded fitness fans, perfecting their running technique, and improving their strength, endurance, aerobic capacity, and flexibility are encouraged to search out running programs in geographic areas that suit their needs. A logical place to start would be local athletic clubs, running magazines that are available at newsstands or through subscription, and even an Internet search.

Runners in front of the Hotel Waldhaus and lake at St. Moritz (one site of the author's running seminars).

178

Index

Index